MW01615615

LIVING LIKE A STOIC

CULTIVATING WISDOM, EMOTIONAL RESILIENCE, POSITIVITY, CONFIDENCE, CALMNESS, AND MEDITATIONS FOR PERSEVERANCE IN TODAY'S MODERN LIFE

MAX STOA

MODERN MIND STOICS

ISBN13: 978-93-5891-026-1 (eBook)

ISBN13: 978-3-0326-0491-0 (paperback)

ISBN13: 978-3-8026-7288-0 (hardcopy)

You have power over your mind — not outside events. Realize this, and you will find strength.

MARCUS AURELIUS

CONTENTS

FOREWORD

I want to start by thanking you for your interest in exploring the profound philosophy of Stoicism with me through this book. This journey is not just about imparting the wisdom of this ancient philosophy, but also about sharing how its principles have subtly but significantly transformed my life.

When I first encountered Stoicism, I was captivated by its profound simplicity. Its core tenets, such as the idea that we cannot control everything that happens to us, but we can control how we respond, resonated deeply within me. In a world where we're constantly bombarded with an overwhelming amount of information and expectations, Stoicism has offered me a sanctuary, a means to find balance and peace.

This book was born from my desire to share the transformative power of Stoicism, particularly with the young minds grappling with life's complexities. Although I have penned this book with a focus on the challenges encountered by today's younger generation, I believe the teachings of Stoicism are universal and can guide anyone seeking clarity and serenity amidst life's turmoil.

Despite being a few millennia old, the lessons from Stoicism are as relevant today as they were when first articulated by the likes of

Marcus Aurelius and Seneca. However, I must clarify, I am not a sage or a scholar; I am a student of Stoicism myself. This book is a collection of insights that I have gained from years of studying and practicing Stoicism, written in a relatable and comprehensible way.

My aim is not to give you prescriptive steps to becoming a perfect Stoic; rather, I hope to spark an interest in Stoic philosophy, encouraging you to explore and incorporate its teachings into your life as you see fit. I truly believe that even a simple understanding of Stoic principles can provide a strong foundation for dealing with life's ups and downs more effectively.

As we embark on this exploration together, I invite you to approach this book with an open mind. Regardless of where you are on your life's journey, the timeless wisdom of Stoicism can provide guidance, comfort, and a fresh perspective. I hope this book will be a valuable companion as you navigate your path to inner peace and resilience.

Thank you for joining me on this journey. Let's dive into the wisdom of Stoicism and unearth the tranquility it holds for us all.

INTRODUCTION

I'm often asked, "Why Stoicism?" The answer is not a simple one. My journey to Stoicism was not a straightforward path, nor was it an overnight transformation. It was an intricate process, one that was seeded in the complex soil of life experiences and personal introspection, and nurtured by continuous learning and application.

From my early years, I noticed a recurring theme in my life - an internal struggle to make sense of the world around me, its unpredictability, and my place in it. Like many, I found myself in the maze of societal pressures, personal expectations, and the innate human quest for happiness and peace. This struggle magnified as I entered adulthood, carrying with me the weight of decisions that seemed to become progressively challenging.

I observed similar challenges among the younger generation. They were grappling with the paradox of choice, the pressures of societal expectations, the relentless pursuit of success, and the resulting stress and dissatisfaction. In a world that is constantly changing and bombarding us with stimuli, it felt like we were losing our capacity to stay grounded, to differentiate what matters from what doesn't, and most importantly, to stay true to ourselves.

It was during one such reflective phase that I stumbled upon

Stoicism. A philosophy that, in its essence, taught equanimity and peace in the face of life's ups and downs. The beauty of Stoicism, to me, lies in its simplicity and practicality. It doesn't promise a life devoid of troubles; rather, it provides a roadmap to navigate them with grace and resilience.

In the beginning, my understanding of Stoicism was superficial, merely a set of abstract concepts. I knew the philosophy but had yet to truly experience it. It was the deliberate decision to practice these principles that marked the real beginning of my stoic journey. Since then, it has been a daily exercise of understanding, introspection, and conscious action.

Though the path hasn't been easy, every moment invested in practicing Stoicism has been worthwhile. I've discovered an inner reservoir of strength I didn't know existed. It has taught me to separate things within my control from those that are not, to accept life as it comes without being swayed by external events, and to remain calm and composed in the face of adversity. It has equipped me with the tools to navigate life's complexities with a degree of tranquility and clarity.

But why write a book about it? There's an African proverb that goes, "If you want to go fast, go alone. If you want to go far, go together." I realized the power of shared understanding and growth. As I began to reap the benefits of Stoicism, I felt a growing desire to share my experiences and insights. This book is a way for me to extend my hand to those who are on a similar journey or are intrigued by the prospect of it.

I don't claim to be a perfect Stoic. If anything, I am more aware of my imperfections now than ever before. But Stoicism, for me, isn't about perfection. It's about progress, about becoming a little better each day than I was the day before. It's about fostering resilience, patience, and compassion, both towards myself and others.

This book, therefore, is a humble attempt to share what I have learned so far. It's about my reflections on the timeless wisdom of Stoic philosophers, my understanding of their teachings, and how I have been applying these principles in my daily life. It's about a philosophy that is as relevant today as it was over two thousand years ago and has the potential to transform lives. It's about a journey, my journey, towards becoming a better version of myself, and inviting you to join me on this path.

I welcome you to join me in this exploration of Stoicism, to question, to learn, and to grow together. Let's embark on this journey with an open mind and a willing heart, nurturing our innate ability to lead a good life, a life of virtue, wisdom, and inner peace.

CHAPTER 1
WHO IS THE BOOK FOR?

As I begin this chapter, I imagine myself sitting across from you, dear reader. You might be a young professional, embarking on your career journey, filled with dreams and ambitions. Or perhaps you are a college student, stepping out into the world, looking at the crossroads of life's many opportunities and choices. Maybe you're someone who's been working for a while, questioning if there's more to life than this relentless hustle. Or, you could be anyone, curious and open-minded, seeking wisdom that can help navigate life's unpredictable waters.

I wrote this book keeping in mind the unique challenges and dilemmas faced by young adults today. In our rapidly changing world, the younger generation experiences a variety of stressors that previous generations might not have encountered. The overwhelming number of choices available can lead to decision fatigue. The struggle to maintain a work-life balance amidst the hustle culture can be daunting. The incessant exposure to the highlight reels of others' lives on social media can trigger feelings of inadequacy and FOMO (Fear of Missing Out).

While this book is especially for you, it doesn't stop there. The beauty of Stoicism is that it transcends age, profession, and cultural boundaries. Its principles are universal, providing a compass that can guide anyone through the highs and lows of life. So, whether you're a student, a professional, a parent, a retiree, or anyone seeking a deeper sense of peace and purpose, this book has something for you.

This book aims to be a guide, a friend, helping you navigate your path. I hope to offer you perspectives that can enable you to differentiate between what is within your control and what is not, to maintain equanimity in the face of both success and failure, to cultivate a deep sense of appreciation for the present moment, and to create your inner citadel of peace amidst the chaos.

I want to emphasize here that this book is not a magic potion. It won't miraculously solve all your problems or immediately eliminate the stressors in your life. What it can do, however, is offer you a different lens to look at these challenges. It can equip you with strategies to handle them more effectively, to minimize the unnecessary stress and anxiety in your life, and to lead a more fulfilled and tranquil existence.

Moreover, it's important to remember that this book is not a one-size-fits-all guide. Everyone's journey with Stoicism will be unique because each of us is unique, with different life experiences, perspectives, and contexts. I encourage you to approach this philosophy with an open mind and a willingness to adapt its principles to your life. Consider this book as a compass rather than a map; it will provide you with the directions, but the path you carve is entirely your own.

I am sharing my understanding and interpretation of Stoicism, rooted in my personal journey. As you read this book, you might agree with some ideas and disagree with others, and that's perfectly okay. The goal is not to have you agree with everything but to inspire thought, reflection, and possibly, transformation.

In conclusion, this book is for anyone who is interested in exploring an ancient yet timeless philosophy, one that has the potential to transform your approach to life and adversity. Whether you're at the beginning of your adult journey or well into it, the wisdom of Stoicism can provide you with tools to navigate life with greater serenity, resilience, and wisdom. I invite you to step into this exploration with an open mind and a curious heart. Here's to our shared journey towards a more fulfilled and tranquil life.

CHAPTER 2
STOICISM: A PHILOSOPHY FOR TODAY

As we delve into the heart of this book, let's first ask the question, "What is Stoicism?" To answer this, we need to journey back in time, to ancient Greece and Rome, where Stoicism was born and flourished.

Stoicism, a school of Hellenistic philosophy, was founded in Athens by Zeno of Citium in the early 3rd century BC. The philosophy received its name from the location where Zeno taught, the 'Stoa Poikile' or 'Painted Porch.' But Stoicism is far more than an academic philosophy confined to the classrooms and the scholarly discourse of the time. It is a practical guide to life.

The Stoics posited that everything around us operates according to a web of cause and effect, resulting in a rational structure of the universe, which they referred to as 'Logos.' While some things are in our control, many others are not. According to the Stoics, our control is limited to our own actions, thoughts, and feelings. Everything else— wealth, fame, health, and other people's actions—is not entirely in our control. They are, in Stoic terminology, 'indifferent.' This is not to say that they don't matter but rather that they should not disturb our inner peace and tranquility.

The core of Stoicism lies in the pursuit of virtue. The Stoics defined virtue as living in accordance with nature, embracing rationality, and focusing on what's truly important. They believed that a virtuous life is a good life, regardless of wealth, power, or other external circumstances. Virtue, to the Stoics, is the highest form of goodness and the only good that is entirely within our control.

Perhaps the most famous Stoic, Roman Emperor Marcus Aurelius, summed it up beautifully in his 'Meditations': "You have power over your mind—not outside events. Realize this, and you will find strength." This succinctly captures the essence of Stoic philosophy: a focus on self-control, resilience, and acceptance of what life presents to us.

But why discuss an ancient philosophy in today's context? What relevance does Stoicism hold in our lives today? As we navigate the challenges and complexities of the modern world, it might seem unlikely that a philosophy conceived over 2000 years ago could offer us any practical wisdom. However, you might be surprised to discover the incredible relevance of Stoic philosophy in our current times.

One of the central tenets of Stoicism is the focus on what we can control and acceptance of what we cannot. Today, we live in a world that is characterized by rapid change and unpredictability. From global issues like climate change and geopolitical instability to personal challenges such as job insecurity or health concerns, we are confronted with situations that can cause significant anxiety and stress. It's in these moments that Stoic philosophy can provide an anchor.

Stoicism teaches us to respond to these external events with equanimity, focusing on our actions and reactions instead of fretting over things outside our control. This practice, when incorporated into our daily lives, can help reduce anxiety, promote mental tranquility, and lead to a more fulfilling life.

By accepting the inevitability of change and uncertainty, we free ourselves from the distress that comes with unmet expectations. Instead of being swayed by every external event or opinion, we can remain centered and maintain our inner peace. This shift in perspective can dramatically alter our approach to life's challenges, fostering resilience and strength in the face of adversity.

Stoicism is not about suppressing emotions; rather, it encourages us to examine them, to question their origin, and to consciously decide whether they are serving our highest good. In an era where we are often driven by fleeting emotions and instant gratification, this is a profound lesson.

As we explore further, we find another core idea of Stoicism - the practice of gratitude and appreciation for the present moment. Today, in our goal-oriented and fast-paced world, we are often so focused on the future, on our next achievement, that we forget to appreciate the present. We might overlook the beauty of the moment, the joy in simple pleasures, and the value of the ordinary. Stoicism invites us to slow down, to savor the present, and to cultivate gratitude for what we have, rather than constantly yearning for what we don't.

Stoicism also provides us with a potent antidote to the prevalent comparison and dissatisfaction culture. Stoic philosophers emphasized the value of self-worth and inner peace over external validation and material success. They taught that true happiness comes from within and is largely independent of external circumstances or others' opinions.

Consider this in the context of our digital age, where we are constantly bombarded with images of 'perfect' lives and achievements on social media, leading to feelings of inadequacy and dissatisfaction. Stoicism can guide us in maintaining our self-esteem and happiness, reminding us that our worth is not defined by external validation but by our virtues and actions.

Furthermore, Stoicism encourages us to see challenges and adversities as opportunities for growth and learning. When confronted with obstacles, instead of viewing them as setbacks, Stoics advise us to reframe them as tests of our character and resilience. This shift in perspective can empower us to face life's hurdles with strength and serenity.

In our current age, where we often seek instant solutions to our problems, Stoicism reminds us of the value of patience and perseverance. It teaches us that growth and wisdom often come through trials and that resilience is a virtue to be cultivated.

Now, you may be wondering, why is it that so many famous and successful people subscribe to Stoicism? From historical figures like

Roman Emperor Marcus Aurelius and philosopher Seneca to contemporary icons like NFL coach Pete Carroll and entrepreneur Tim Ferriss, a wide array of individuals from various fields have drawn upon Stoic philosophy.

The reason for this, I believe, is that Stoicism provides a solid foundation for handling success and failure. It equips us with the tools to maintain humility in success and resilience in failure. It helps us keep our ego in check, remain focused on our goals, and navigate the complexities of life with grace and composure.

As we delve deeper into Stoicism in the following chapters, I invite you to keep an open mind. Stoicism is not a rigid doctrine but a set of guiding principles that can be adapted to our individual circumstances and needs. I encourage you to take from it what resonates with you and apply it in a way that best serves your journey.

To dispel a potential misconception, this book is not just another self-help book in the sea of self-help literature. While it does aim to guide and assist, it doesn't offer quick fixes or effortless solutions to life's problems. Instead, it offers a framework for understanding and navigating life's complexities, a philosophy that promotes self-reflection, personal growth, and resilience.

By now, you may have started to see why Stoicism has gained such popularity and why it is more relevant today than ever. In a world that is increasingly complex and stressful, Stoicism provides a beacon of tranquility, guiding us towards a more serene, virtuous, and fulfilling life.

I hope this chapter has given you a glimpse of what Stoicism is, its historical context, and its relevance in our lives today. As we continue this journey, I look forward to sharing more about this powerful philosophy and how it has transformed my life and could transform yours too.

We've discussed the roots of Stoicism, its core tenets, and its relevance to our contemporary lives. Yet, we've barely scratched the surface of this profound philosophy. But before we delve deeper, let's address another important question – why should we follow Stoicism?

One of the key reasons is the peace of mind it promises. By focusing on what's in our control and accepting what's not, we can significantly reduce our anxiety and stress. This doesn't mean that we become passive observers of life. Instead, it empowers us to channel our energy into areas where we can make a real impact, thus leading to a more fulfilling and effective life.

Another reason to follow Stoicism is its practicality. Unlike some philosophical doctrines that are abstract and hard to implement, Stoicism is very much a practical philosophy. Its teachings can be applied in our daily lives, helping us navigate both minor irritations and major challenges. It is a philosophy designed for action and for life.

Stoicism also promotes resilience and mental toughness. It teaches us that hardships and adversity are a part of life, and instead of running away from them, we can use them as opportunities for growth and self-improvement. This reframing of challenges can make us stronger, more resilient, and better equipped to handle life's ups and downs.

Furthermore, Stoicism encourages a simpler, more focused life. In our consumer-driven society, where we're often pushed towards acquiring more and achieving more, Stoicism reminds us of the value of simplicity and contentment. It teaches us to appreciate what we have and focus on our internal virtues rather than external possessions or status. This can lead to a more satisfied, less cluttered life.

Lastly, but importantly, Stoicism can make us better human beings. It emphasizes virtues like wisdom, courage, justice, and temperance. By striving to embody these virtues, we can improve our interactions with others, make better decisions, and lead a more ethical, meaningful life.

These are just a few of the reasons to follow Stoicism. The true beauty of this philosophy lies in its adaptability and its potential to provide guidance and comfort in various aspects of life. As we journey further into the realm of Stoicism, you will discover many more reasons why this ancient philosophy is worth exploring and integrating into your life.

At this juncture, I want to clarify a crucial point: I don't consider myself a true Stoic. I am a student of Stoicism, learning and practicing its principles daily to navigate my life's voyage. I have found tremendous value in this philosophy, and I believe that it can offer similar benefits to many others. That's why I chose to share my understanding and interpretation of Stoicism through this book.

In the following chapters, we will explore the wisdom of Stoicism in more detail. We will delve into the teachings of renowned Stoic philosophers, examine their relevance to our lives, and discuss how we can apply them practically. This exploration is not just about understanding Stoicism intellectually but about integrating it into our daily lives.

As we embark on this journey together, I invite you to approach it with curiosity, openness, and patience. Stoicism is not a quick fix, and understanding its depths may take time. But I assure you, the rewards are well worth the journey.

The goal of this book is not to turn you into a Stoic overnight but to offer you a different perspective on life, a toolkit for dealing with challenges, and a pathway towards a more tranquil, virtuous, and fulfilled existence. So, let's embark on this exciting journey together, and may we all find the strength, peace, and wisdom we seek in the timeless philosophy of Stoicism.

Here's to our shared exploration of Stoicism – a philosophy for today, and every day.

CHAPTER 3

THE FOUR CARDINAL VIRTUES: THE PILLARS OF STOIC PHILOSOPHY

The Four Cardinal Virtues - Wisdom, Courage, Justice, and Temperance, serve as the foundational pillars of Stoic philosophy. They embody the ethical standards and moral compass guiding the Stoics towards virtuous living. The Stoics believed that true happiness is achieved when we align our actions with these virtues. In the pursuit of an enlightened and fulfilling life, these virtues shape our attitudes, influence our actions, and steer our decision-making. This chapter aims to delve into each of these cardinal virtues, providing a clear understanding of their significance in Stoicism and their practical application in our daily lives.

WISDOM

In the Stoic philosophy, wisdom is considered the chief virtue, as it is the guiding force that enables us to distinguish between right and wrong, good and bad. It's an understanding of the fundamental nature of reality and the ability to navigate life's complexities with a clear and composed mind. Wisdom is not just the possession of knowledge; it's the judicious application of that knowledge.

To the Stoics, wisdom is an active and continuous process of learning and understanding, not a static state. It encompasses logical thinking, awareness of our ignorance, and a lifelong commitment to seeking truth. It encourages us to question, to learn, and to grow, while equipping us with the tools to deal with life's uncertainties.

The Stoics divided wisdom into three parts: the wisdom to handle things as they come, the wisdom to handle things before they happen, and the wisdom to distinguish between what we can control and what we can't. It's the rational understanding that our control is limited to our own actions and reactions, not external events or outcomes.

In practice, Stoic wisdom is evident in our daily decision-making. It helps us navigate through the complexities of life, such as managing relationships, dealing with adversity, or making ethical choices. It prompts us to act with reason and clarity, rather than being swayed by emotions or misconceptions.

Let's consider a relatable example. Imagine you're stuck in a traffic jam, and you're getting late for a meeting. A typical response might involve stress, frustration, or even anger. But the Stoic approach, informed by wisdom, would be different. It recognizes that the traffic is beyond your control, but your reaction to it is within your control. Instead of succumbing to stress or anger, you could use the time to listen to a podcast, plan your day, or simply appreciate the moment of quiet in your busy day.

Wisdom, in this context, doesn't eliminate the traffic jam or magically transport you to your meeting. Instead, it changes your perception of the situation and your reaction to it. It takes a moment of stress and frustration and turns it into an opportunity for personal growth and learning.

This anecdote captures the essence of Stoic wisdom in a nutshell: It's not about controlling external circumstances, but about understanding and managing our internal responses. As we continue our exploration of the Four Cardinal Virtues, you'll see that wisdom serves as the foundation for the other virtues: courage, justice, and temperance. Each of these virtues, applied individually and collectively, guides us on our journey toward a more Stoic life.

This understanding of wisdom and its applications paves the way for us to consider the next virtue - courage. Wisdom and courage, together, enable us to face life's challenges head-on, fully aware of our limitations but ready to act in alignment with our principles. As we move to the next section, we delve deeper into the virtue of courage and how it intertwines with wisdom to create a harmonious Stoic life.

COURAGE

Courage, from the Stoic viewpoint, moves beyond the common understanding of being brave in the face of physical danger. While physical bravery does fall under the umbrella of courage, the Stoics placed higher emphasis on moral and intellectual courage – the courage to stand up for what's right and the bravery to question, challenge, and change our deeply held beliefs.

In the Stoic philosophy, courage is the virtuous middle between the extremes of recklessness and cowardice. It involves making a stand not because it is the easy thing to do, but because it is the right thing to do, even if it leads to personal discomfort or societal disapproval.

One significant aspect of Stoic courage is the bravery to face and accept the truth, even if it is unsettling or inconvenient. This could be the truth about ourselves, our circumstances, or the world at large. Stoic courage compels us to confront these truths, question our biases, and reassess our beliefs, even if it means stepping out of our comfort zones or acknowledging our flaws.

For instance, consider the example of a high-ranking executive in a corporate firm who discovers unethical practices within the company. Stoic courage in this situation involves not only acknowledging this uncomfortable truth but also standing up against the wrongdoing, despite the risk of facing backlash or losing the job.

Moreover, Stoic courage helps us face life's adversities with resilience and determination. Whether we're dealing with personal setbacks, health issues, or loss, Stoic courage inspires us to endure these hardships without surrendering to fear or despair. It encourages acceptance of things beyond our control, while empowering us to handle our challenges with fortitude and grace.

Marcus Aurelius, a Stoic philosopher and Roman Emperor, once said, "You have power over your mind – not outside events. Realize this, and you will find strength." This quote encapsulates the essence of Stoic courage – the recognition that our power lies not in avoiding hardships but in confronting them with a composed and resilient mind.

Finally, Stoic courage intertwines with the virtue of wisdom. Wisdom equips us with the discernment to identify what is within our control and what is not. Courage empowers us to accept and handle both with equanimity and resolve. Together, wisdom and courage lay the groundwork for the next virtue in our exploration: justice.

As we dive into the next section, we will delve into the Stoic understanding of justice and how it, along with wisdom and courage, contributes to the pursuit of a virtuous life.

JUSTICE

Justice, as seen by the Stoics, encompasses more than just the legal definition of the term; it refers to the broader principle of living in harmony with others, treating everyone with fairness, kindness, and understanding. Justice in Stoicism instructs us to perform our duties to society responsibly and to respect the inherent dignity and worth of every individual.

In the Stoic framework, justice is closely tied to empathy and compassion. The Stoics viewed all human beings as fundamentally interconnected, a single community bound by reason and mutual obligation. They asserted that it is our duty to respect this interconnectedness by treating others not merely as means to our ends, but as ends in themselves, deserving of respect and kindness.

For example, Stoic justice would guide a school teacher to not just impart knowledge, but also to foster a supportive, inclusive, and fair environment for all students, irrespective of their background or abilities. This could involve extra effort to assist students who are struggling or creating an atmosphere that encourages participation and respects diverse opinions.

In a societal context, justice guides us towards recognizing and challenging social injustices. It may involve standing against discriminatory practices, advocating for equal opportunities, or contributing to causes that address social inequality. Epictetus, a Stoic philosopher, emphasized this aspect when he said, "What you would avoid suffering yourself, seek not to impose on others."

Furthermore, Stoic justice involves honesty and integrity. It implies standing by truth and fairness, even if it might lead to unfavorable outcomes for ourselves. A simple illustration would be a sports player who admits to a mistake, even if it costs the game, because upholding fairness is more valuable than winning unjustly.

Stoic justice isn't merely reactive, but proactive. It is not only about treating others fairly when we interact with them but also about actively seeking to make the world a more just place. This could mean volunteering for a cause, mentoring someone in need, or simply being more understanding and patient in our daily interactions.

On a personal level, Stoic justice encourages us to be fair with ourselves as well. It asks us to be honest in our self-assessment, acknowledge our faults, and work on improving ourselves, but without undue harshness or self-condemnation. In this way, justice links with wisdom, courage, and the final Stoic virtue we will explore next: temperance.

In the next section, we will unravel how temperance, intertwined with wisdom, courage, and justice, creates a balanced and harmonious life as envisioned by the Stoics. As we move forward, we'll see how these virtues are not standalone concepts, but deeply interlinked, each one enriching and enabling the other.

TEMPERANCE

Temperance, as understood by the Stoics, signifies a disciplined and moderate approach to life. It doesn't mean total abstinence or severe self-denial; rather, it refers to a measured way of living where choices are influenced by reason, not by unchecked desires or impulses. Temperance is about maintaining a balanced state of mind and behavior, resisting the pull towards excess.

The Stoic philosophy, like other ancient Greek philosophies, promotes the idea of the 'Golden Mean' - finding the middle ground between deficiency and excess. It's the virtue that helps us navigate through life without being swayed by extreme emotions, desires, or actions. Temperance holds the other virtues - wisdom, courage, and justice - in equilibrium, ensuring none outweighs the other.

To illustrate, imagine the scenario of dining at a lavish buffet. An absence of temperance might lead to gluttony, driven by desire to taste every dish, which may result in discomfort or ill-health. Total abstinence, on the other hand, might mean not eating at all, denying oneself the enjoyment of food. The Stoic approach, guided by temperance, would be to enjoy the meal, sampling a variety of dishes but stopping at the point of satiety, not overindulgence.

Temperance applies to other areas of life too. In the realm of work, it is the virtue that helps us find balance between overwork and idleness, promoting a healthy work-life balance. In relationships, it guides us to express and manage our emotions in a balanced way, avoiding outbursts of anger or excessive dependence on others. In our consumer-driven society, temperance encourages us to resist the allure of unnecessary material possessions, focusing instead on what truly adds value to our lives.

A great Stoic example of temperance is the philosopher Seneca. Despite being one of the wealthiest men in Rome, he practiced a lifestyle of simplicity and moderation, eschewing extravagant displays of wealth. He would regularly practice poverty to remind himself of what truly mattered and to maintain a balanced perspective on life.

In our modern world, temperance could mean limiting our screen time, moderating our consumption of news or social media, maintaining a balanced diet, or setting boundaries in our professional and personal lives. It's about making informed, rational decisions that align with our core values and contribute to our well-being and growth.

Remember, temperance is not about depriving ourselves, but about making choices that truly serve our best interests. It requires a deep understanding of ourselves, our needs, and our values. It's a virtue that encourages us to lead a life of quality, not just quantity.

With this, we conclude our exploration of the four cardinal virtues of Stoicism: wisdom, courage, justice, and temperance. Each of these virtues contributes to a fulfilling, resilient, and harmonious life. They guide us to live according to reason and virtue, helping us navigate life's challenges with serenity and integrity.

In the next part of our Stoic journey, we'll delve deeper into how to apply these virtues in daily life, providing practical exercises and reflections to integrate Stoicism into our modern existence. Until then, remember the words of Marcus Aurelius, "Just that you do the right thing. The rest doesn't matter."

————

As we conclude this exploration into the four cardinal virtues of Stoicism - wisdom, courage, justice, and temperance - it's clear to see how they intricately weave together to form the foundation of the Stoic philosophy and provide a framework for leading a fulfilled, resilient, and balanced life.

These virtues aren't isolated elements; rather, they intersect and influence one another, creating a harmonious blend. Wisdom equips us with the discernment to make reasoned decisions, courage empowers us to act on those decisions, justice ensures our actions are fair and beneficial to others, and temperance maintains the equilibrium, preventing any single aspect from overshadowing the rest.

Each virtue plays a crucial role, yet none can stand alone. Their true power is realized when they are practiced in unison, guiding us towards a life led by virtue and reason, not swayed by external circumstances or internal disturbances.

As we navigate the complexities of our modern world, these ancient virtues still hold immense relevance. They beckon us to delve deeper, to question, to reflect and to act not just for our benefit, but for the betterment of all. In each decision we make, in every interaction we have, these virtues can guide us.

As we leave you with these thoughts, we encourage you to contemplate these virtues in your own life. Reflect on your actions, your decisions, and your interactions with others. Where can you see these virtues playing out? Where can you implement them more fully? Remember, Stoicism is not just a philosophy to be understood, but a way of life to be lived.

In the words of Epictetus, "Don't explain your philosophy. Embody it." As we continue on this Stoic journey, let us strive to not just understand these virtues, but to embody them, integrating them into our daily lives, allowing them to shape us into better, more virtuous individuals.

Next, we will delve deeper into the application of these virtues.

———

REFLECTION/ACTIONABLE TASKS:

Understanding the virtues of Stoicism is just the beginning. True transformation occurs when we apply these teachings in our daily lives. Here are some self-reflective questions and actionable tasks to help you incorporate these Stoic virtues into your journey:

Wisdom

Reflective question: Consider a recent situation where you made a decision. How did you come to that conclusion? What role did wisdom play?

Action: Set aside 10 minutes each day for quiet reflection. Use this time to consider the decisions you made and whether they were guided by wisdom.

Courage

Reflective question: Think of an instance where you showed courage. It could be standing up for someone, voicing your opinion, or confronting a fear.

Action: Identify one fear or challenge you're facing currently. How can you apply the virtue of courage to confront this?

Justice

Reflective question: Can you recall a situation where you were fair even though it was easier to be unjust? How did it make you feel?

Action: The next time you're in a disagreement, strive to understand the other person's perspective before making a judgment.

Temperance

Reflective question: Reflect on your lifestyle and habits. Are there any extremes that you could moderate for a more balanced life?

Action: Choose one area of your life where you could practice more temperance. It could be diet, technology use, or work-life balance.

Reflect on these questions and tasks over the next week. Write down your thoughts and observations in a journal. Remember, the purpose of these exercises is not to judge yourself but to become more aware and integrate these virtues into your everyday life.

In the Stoic tradition, virtue is not an end point but a journey. Each step you take brings you closer to embodying the wisdom, courage, justice, and temperance that were so valued by the ancient Stoics. And in doing so, you create a life of tranquility, resilience, and true fulfillment.

CHAPTER 4

DEMYSTIFYING STOIC WISDOM: INTERPRETATIONS OF TEN FAMOUS QUOTES

Throughout my journey with Stoicism, one of the aspects that resonated deeply with me was the timeless wisdom encapsulated in Stoic quotes. These nuggets of wisdom have guided, comforted, and inspired me in various phases of life. They have provided me with a compass to navigate life's complexities and a touchstone to ground myself in moments of confusion or turmoil.

In this chapter, I want to share ten of these Stoic quotes that have had a profound impact on me. I will not only share the quote itself but also my understanding and interpretation of each quote. My aim is not to provide an academic dissection of these quotes but to share a relatable, jargon-free interpretation that can be easily understood and applied by all readers.

It's essential to remember that these interpretations are personal they are based on my journey, my experiences, and my understanding of Stoicism. You may find different meanings in these quotes, and that's perfectly okay. Stoicism is a personal philosophy, and its teachings can resonate differently with different people.

So, let's embark on this journey of exploration, of delving into the wisdom of Stoic philosophers, of interpreting their teachings in a way that is meaningful and applicable to our lives. And remember, the goal is not to memorize these quotes, but to internalize their wisdom, to let them guide us in our actions and decisions, to allow them to transform our perspective and enrich our lives.

"We suffer more often in imagination than in reality."

SENECA

This quote from Seneca, a renowned Stoic philosopher, speaks volumes about the human condition. It highlights how we often create our own suffering through our thoughts, fears, and expectations. We worry about the future, dwell on the past, fear loss or failure, and all this mental activity causes us stress and suffering. In reality, the events or circumstances we dread often don't occur or are less severe than we imagined. By understanding this, we can learn to control our imagination, live more in the present, and reduce our suffering.

"You have power over your mind - not outside events. Realize this, and you will find strength."

MARCUS AURELIUS

Marcus Aurelius, a Roman Emperor and one of the most famous Stoic philosophers, reminds us in this quote that our power lies in controlling our mind, not external events. We often cannot control what happens around us, but we can control how we respond to it. This realization can be liberating and empowering, allowing us to face life's ups and downs with strength and equanimity.

"He who fears death will never do anything worth of a man who is alive."

SENECA

This profound insight by Seneca highlights the debilitating effect of fearing death. If we spend our lives in the shadow of death, constantly fearing its inevitability, we prevent ourselves from truly living. Instead, by accepting death as a part of life, we can free ourselves from this fear and pursue a life of value and meaning.

"Difficulty is what wakes up the genius."

NASSIM NICHOLAS TALEB

While Nassim Nicholas Taleb is not a Stoic philosopher, this quote embodies Stoic principles perfectly. Challenges and difficulties, according to Stoicism, are not hindrances but opportunities to grow, learn, and bring out our inner strength. They awaken our potential and spur us to become better versions of ourselves.

"It's not what happens to you, but how you react to it that matters."

EPICTETUS

Epictetus, a Greek Stoic philosopher, brings our attention to the importance of our reactions. Events in themselves are neutral; it's our perception and response to them that give them their value or power over us. By learning to respond wisely and constructively, we can better manage the events in our lives.

"He who laughs at himself never runs out of things to laugh at."

EPICTETUS

A touch of humor and the ability to laugh at oneself, suggests Epictetus, can make life more enjoyable. It allows us to take ourselves less seriously, easing stress and promoting a more balanced perspective on life.

"Waste no more time arguing what a good man should be. Be one."

MARCUS AURELIUS

Marcus Aurelius reminds us that virtue and morality are not just theoretical concepts to be debated but practical qualities to be embodied. Instead of discussing or judging what constitutes a good person, we should strive to become one through our actions.

"The obstacle in the path becomes the path. Never forget, within every obstacle is an opportunity to improve our condition."

RYAN HOLIDAY

In his book 'The Obstacle Is the Way', Ryan Holiday, a modern advocate of Stoicism, highlights the Stoic approach to challenges. Obstacles, rather than being barriers, can become the path forward, providing opportunities for growth, learning, and improvement.

"Man is disturbed not by things, but by the views he takes of them."

EPICTETUS

Epictetus underlines the power of perspective in this quote. We are not disturbed by events themselves, but by our interpretation of them. By changing our perspective, we can change our emotional response to events and reduce our disturbance.

"If it is not right, do not do it, if it is not true, do not say it."

MARCUS AURELIUS

Marcus Aurelius lays out a simple but powerful principle for ethical behavior. If an action or statement does not align with righteousness or truth, we should abstain from it. This principle can guide us in making ethical decisions and living a virtuous life.

These quotes are just a small glimpse into the profound wisdom of Stoicism. In the following chapters, we will explore and delve into the lives of the philosophers who penned these quotes, their historical context, and their practical implications for our lives.

CHAPTER 5
EXPLORING THE LIVES AND TEACHINGS OF STOIC PHILOSOPHERS

The Stoic philosophy we know and appreciate today is not the result of a single individual's effort. It is a product of a multitude of wise thinkers who dedicated their lives to examining the nature of existence and sharing their insights on living a virtuous life. Each Stoic philosopher we are about to explore has made unique contributions to this practical philosophy, enriching it with their experiences, wisdom, and teachings.

In the following chapters, we will explore the lives and teachings of some of the most influential Stoic philosophers. From Epictetus, the slave-turned-philosopher, to Marcus Aurelius, the philosopher emperor, to Seneca, the influential statesman, each philosopher has added a new layer of depth to Stoicism.

We will delve into the lives of these philosophers. We will journey back in time, exploring the era they lived in, the challenges they faced, and how their experiences shaped their philosophical views. Understanding the historical and personal context of these philosophers will offer us a deeper appreciation of their wisdom.

For instance, when we understand that Epictetus began his life as a slave, his teachings on the power of the mind and the importance of focusing on what we can control gain a new level of profundity. When we appreciate that Marcus Aurelius was an emperor, his insights on virtue, duty, and the insignificance of external validation reflect a remarkable depth of wisdom and self-awareness.

We will also delve into what inspired these philosophers to walk the path of Stoicism. Was it a personal tragedy, a quest for understanding, or the influence of another philosopher? Knowing what drew them towards Stoicism and how it shaped their lives can provide us with valuable lessons on how to incorporate this philosophy into our own lives.

Each philosopher, despite living in different times and circumstances, shared a common thread – a commitment to the Stoic principles of wisdom, courage, justice, and temperance. As we explore their lives and teachings, you will notice the echoes of these principles in their quotes, their philosophies, and their actions.

Remember, the goal of these explorations is not merely intellectual understanding. It is to draw inspiration from their lives and teachings, to see how Stoic philosophy can be applied in diverse circumstances, and to use this wisdom to guide our own lives.

In the next chapters, we will begin this journey of exploration, starting with Epictetus. A philosopher who, despite his early life of hardship, transformed his experiences into teachings of timeless wisdom. Let's delve into his life, explore his philosophy, and learn from his wisdom.

As we move through the book, you'll discover that each philosopher, while rooted in the core principles of Stoicism, brought a unique perspective to the philosophy. Seneca's eloquent essays provide us with practical advice on dealing with anger, grief, and the shortness of life. Marcus Aurelius' meditations, often written in the quiet solitude of the night, ponder the transient nature of life and the importance of duty and virtue.

On the other hand, Epictetus' teachings, delivered through his discourses and manual (Enchiridion), focus on the dichotomy of control and how this understanding forms the basis of a good life.

Each chapter dedicated to a philosopher will not only familiarize you with their unique viewpoint but also help you understand the evolution of Stoic philosophy. From its early days in the streets of

Athens to its current global resurgence, Stoicism has continued to adapt and provide guidance to seekers of wisdom.

While Stoicism encourages us to learn from the past and prepare for the future, it also emphasizes living in the present. I hope that the insights gained from these chapters will help you live a more content, balanced, and meaningful life today. I believe that every reader will resonate with at least one philosopher, one quote, or one piece of wisdom that will make a difference in their lives.

Finally, I want to remind you that while these philosophers may seem extraordinary, they were people just like us. They faced adversity, struggled with their weaknesses, and sought to better themselves. Their wisdom is not beyond our reach. Their teachings are not locked in the past. They are here, in this book, waiting to be discovered and used by you.

In the upcoming chapters, let's dig deeper into the teachings and lives of significant Stoic philosophers. As we navigate through their stories and insights, we will continue to uncover the depth and breadth of Stoic wisdom, appreciating its potential to guide and enrich our lives.

CHAPTER 6

EPICTETUS - THE SLAVE TURNED PHILOSOPHER

E pictetus, a seminal figure in Stoic philosophy, lived a life that was in stark contrast to many of his philosophical contemporaries. Born into slavery around 50 AD in Hierapolis, Phrygia (present-day Pamukkale, Turkey), his early experiences were far removed from the relative luxury enjoyed by other influential Stoics such as Marcus Aurelius. Nevertheless, it was these harsh experiences that helped shape Epictetus into the highly respected philosopher we remember today.

Epictetus's Greek name, which translates to "acquired" or "gained," was likely given to him by his master, implying a rather impersonal and property-based relationship. Despite this harsh beginning, Epictetus's life took a remarkable turn when he became the slave of a wealthy and powerful freedman named Epaphroditos, who served as secretary to the infamous Roman Emperor Nero. It was Epaphroditos who recognized Epictetus's intellectual prowess and sent him to study under the renowned Stoic teacher, Musonius Rufus. This marked the beginning of Epictetus's journey into Stoicism, a journey that would eventually see him become one of the most influential Stoic philosophers of all time.

Epictetus was eventually freed after Emperor Nero's death, and he went on to establish his own philosophy school in Nicopolis, Greece. Here, he spent the rest of his life teaching, writing, and living according to the Stoic principles he had adopted. Epictetus's philosophy was distinctive for its emphasis on ethics and the practice of virtue. He upheld the core Stoic belief that while we cannot control external events, we can control our responses to them. His teachings were practical and actionable, designed to guide individuals on how to live a virtuous and fulfilling life.

His philosophical thoughts and teachings were immortalized in the 'Discourses' and the 'Enchiridion' (The Handbook), although interestingly, Epictetus himself never wrote anything down. Instead, it was one of his students, Arrian, who took it upon himself to record and compile his master's teachings.

Epictetus's influence on Stoicism and, by extension, on the entire Western philosophical tradition, is immense. His teachings have been widely studied and referenced by countless individuals throughout history - from philosophers and writers to leaders and scholars. Even today, his words resonate with those seeking practical wisdom on how to live a good life. Epictetus wasn't just a philosopher who theorized about life; he was a philosopher who provided a roadmap on how to live it.

The life and teachings of Epictetus serve as a vivid testament to the transformative power of Stoic philosophy. Here was a man who rose from the shackles of slavery to become one of the most revered philosophers of his time, demonstrating that the human spirit's potential to rise above adversity and cultivate wisdom knows no bounds. The lessons Epictetus imparted centuries ago continue to inspire and guide us in our quest for personal growth and self-mastery, affirming his place as one of Stoicism's most significant proponents.

EARLY LIFE AND PATH TO STOICISM

Epictetus's beginnings were exceptionally humble, even tragic by some measures. Born into slavery around 50 AD in the city of Hierapolis in ancient Phrygia, Epictetus would experience firsthand the harsh realities of life. Hierapolis, a city known for its hot springs and vast necropolis, was far from the intellectual centers of the ancient world, like Athens or Rome, but it would be the birthplace of one of Stoicism's most influential figures.

As a young slave in Rome, Epictetus served Epaphroditos, a wealthy freedman and secretary to Nero, the notorious Roman Emperor. This would prove to be a defining relationship in Epictetus's life. Despite his lowly status, Epictetus was fortunate in one respect: his master, Epaphroditos, recognized his intellectual potential and allowed him to pursue an education in philosophy.

Epictetus was sent to study under Musonius Rufus, a respected Stoic philosopher. Rufus was known for his belief that philosophy should be practical, an idea that deeply influenced Epictetus. From Rufus, Epictetus learned not just about Stoic philosophy but also about the art of living. It is likely that his status as a slave intensified his understanding and adoption of Stoicism, a philosophy that emphasizes the differentiation between what we can control (our mind and responses) and what we cannot (external circumstances).

Epictetus's early life experiences played a significant role in his philosophical outlook. Having lived under the arbitrary power of others, he understood the fundamental Stoic tenet that external events are beyond our control, but how we respond to them is within our power. As a slave, he learned to apply Stoic principles to cope with his circumstances, focusing on maintaining his inner peace and dignity despite external adversity.

Stoicism became not just a philosophy for Epictetus but a lifeline, shaping his worldview and his approach to life. His teachings reflect his experiences, emphasizing the need to accept life's hardships and focus on cultivating virtue and wisdom. His early life as a slave wasn't a barrier to his philosophical pursuits; instead, it served as a unique backdrop against which his understanding of Stoicism was honed. His resilience in the face of adversity made his teachings all the more credible and powerful.

The emancipation of Epictetus after Nero's death marked a new chapter in his life, where he became a prominent Stoic philosopher in his own right. As a freedman, he continued to delve deeper into Stoicism, ultimately establishing his philosophy school in Nicopolis,

Greece. There, he attracted a broad range of students, from wealthy Romans to aspiring philosophers, all eager to learn the practical wisdom he offered. His journey from slave to respected philosopher is a testament to the transformative power of Stoic philosophy.

As we delve deeper into the life and teachings of Epictetus, it's essential to remember that his understanding of Stoicism was forged in the crucible of personal hardship. His life is a vivid example of Stoic philosophy put into practice, illustrating how a philosophy born in the halls of Athens could be lived out in the most challenging circumstances. It also emphasizes that wisdom, dignity, and tranquility of mind are accessible to everyone, regardless of their social status or life circumstances.

EPICTETUS AS A PHILOSOPHER

Epictetus's journey as a philosopher is truly a testament to the transformative power of Stoic philosophy. His teachings, which center on the power of the individual mind to overcome adversity, are imbued with his unique experience and profound wisdom. Epictetus didn't write any philosophical texts himself; rather, his pupil Arrian documented his teachings in a work known as the "Discourses" and a condensed version called the "Enchiridion," or "Handbook." These works provide invaluable insights into the core principles of Epictetus's Stoic philosophy and his distinctive contributions to this philosophical tradition.

One of the most distinct features of Epictetus's philosophy is the emphasis on the dichotomy of control. He argued that understanding the difference between things that are within our control (our own thoughts and actions) and those that are not (events in the world, other people's actions) is the key to a good life. In his teachings, he says, "We should always be asking ourselves: 'Is this something that is, or is not, in my control?'" This idea is a fundamental principle of Stoic philosophy, and Epictetus's teachings bring it to life in a profoundly powerful way.

Epictetus also made significant contributions to Stoic ethics, focusing on virtue as the highest good. He believed that while we cannot control external events, we can control our character and actions, which should always be directed toward virtue. "It's not what happens to you, but how you react to it that matters," Epictetus famously said, capturing the essence of his ethical teachings. He argued that by practicing virtue and self-discipline, we can maintain tranquility and happiness regardless of external circumstances.

Furthermore, Epictetus's philosophy is characterized by its practicality. He believed that philosophy should not merely be a theoretical exercise but a guide for living a good life. He stressed the importance of applying philosophical principles in daily life, stating, "Don't explain your philosophy. Embody it." This focus on practical wisdom and action is a central feature of Stoic philosophy, and Epictetus's teachings embody it fully.

Epictetus's teachings had a significant impact on the development and spread of Stoic philosophy. His philosophy school in Nicopolis attracted students from all walks of life, helping to disseminate Stoic ideas far and wide. Moreover, the texts produced by his pupil Arrian have served as a critical source of Stoic philosophy for generations of readers. They bring together the central ideas of Stoicism in a practical and accessible form, capturing the enduring relevance of this philosophical tradition.

Through his teachings, Epictetus showed how Stoic philosophy can provide a roadmap for living a meaningful and fulfilled life, irrespective of one's external circumstances. His philosophy offers a compelling vision of human freedom and resilience, grounded in the understanding that our true power lies in our capacity to cultivate virtue and wisdom, regardless of external events. This vision continues to resonate with people worldwide, making Epictetus one of the most influential figures in the Stoic tradition.

Epictetus's philosophy was also characterized by a strong emphasis on personal responsibility and agency. He believed that we are the authors of our own happiness or misery, depending on how we perceive and respond to circumstances. In his discourses, he often stressed, "It's not things that upset us, but our judgement about things." According to him, events in themselves are neutral. It's our judgments about them that cause us distress or joy. This cognitive approach to emotions marks a cornerstone in his philosophical teach-

ings, providing a practical strategy for managing emotional disturbances and achieving equanimity.

While many Stoic principles can seem abstract, Epictetus had a
knack for grounding them in relatable terms. His analogies and
metaphors brought Stoicism to life, connecting profound philosophical
ideas with ordinary experiences. For example, he likened life to a festi-
val, arranged for our benefit by the gods, where we are given the
opportunity to play our part before it's time to leave. By viewing life
through this lens, Epictetus argued we could appreciate our existence
without clinging to it, thereby cultivating a sense of gratitude and
acceptance.

Notably, Epictetus's teachings also highlight the importance of
education and lifelong learning. Despite his initial circumstances as a
slave, he became one of the most renowned philosophers of his time.
His journey emphasizes his belief in education as a tool for personal
growth and transformation. He once stated, "Only the educated are
free," signifying the liberating power of knowledge and the importance
of continuous learning in leading a fulfilling life.

Lastly, Epictetus's teachings extended to the social realm. He taught
his students the importance of fulfilling social roles and responsibilities
with integrity and virtue. From the perspective of Epictetus, one's duty
as a parent, friend, or citizen is an opportunity to practice virtue and
contribute to the common good.

Epictetus's role as a philosopher was not just to expound on Stoic
principles but to live them. His life exemplified the Stoic ideal of inner
peace and resilience in the face of adversity. His journey from a slave to
a revered philosopher provided a real-world testament to the transformative power of Stoicism, reinforcing the universality and practicality
of its teachings. His philosophy and teachings continue to echo across
centuries, guiding individuals towards a path of wisdom, virtue, and
serenity.

EPICTETUS'S PHILOSOPHY AND ITS IMPACT

Epictetus's philosophy was groundbreaking for its time and continues
to hold immense relevance today. His teachings, as passed down

through his pupil Arrian, center around themes of acceptance, control, and individual responsibility, contributing significantly to the foundations of Stoic philosophy. To fully grasp his influence, let's delve into some of his most impactful quotes and teachings.

One of Epictetus's most renowned statements is: "It's not things that upset us, but our judgement about things." This statement is a cornerstone of Stoic philosophy, encapsulating the Stoic approach to emotion management. According to Epictetus, our reactions and emotions result from our judgments and interpretations, not the events themselves. In the face of adversity, we have the power to choose our response. By focusing on our interpretations rather than the events themselves, we can control our emotional reactions and maintain tranquility.

This idea resonates with modern psychological approaches, particularly cognitive-behavioral therapy (CBT), which posits that our thoughts (cognitions) about an event influence our emotional response. From this perspective, Epictetus's philosophy offers a timeless insight into human psychology and emotion regulation.

Another fundamental teaching from Epictetus is his dichotomy of control, best summarized by his quote, "Some things are in our control and others not." This teaching encourages a focus on elements within our power—such as our actions, judgments, and responses—and a detachment from those outside it, like other people's opinions or unforeseen events. The aim is to invest energy in what we can change and accept what we cannot, promoting serenity and efficacy in our lives.

Epictetus's teachings also promote personal integrity and authenticity, emphasizing the importance of living in alignment with one's values and wisdom. In his words, "Don't explain your philosophy. Embody it." Here, Epictetus encourages us to live our philosophy, not just intellectualize it, fostering a shift from abstract contemplation to concrete action. This emphasis on applied philosophy aligns with the Stoic aim to cultivate virtue and wisdom through consistent practice.

From a personal standpoint, these teachings have deepened my understanding of Stoic philosophy, demonstrating its practical relevance and timeless wisdom. Epictetus's ideas provide tangible strategies for emotional resilience, personal effectiveness, and authentic living. By emphasizing control, responsibility, and application, Epictetus illuminates the path towards a more serene and meaningful life. His teachings remind us of the power of perspective and the importance of aligning our actions with our philosophical beliefs. Through these insights, Epictetus contributes significantly to the Stoic aim to live wisely, justly, and in harmony with nature.

These are just a few examples of Epictetus's influential teachings. His philosophical contributions extend far beyond these points, addressing a range of life's challenges and existential questions. Despite being rooted in ancient wisdom, Epictetus's philosophy continues to resonate with modern audiences, offering practical strategies for mental resilience, personal growth, and meaningful living. Through his teachings, we gain a deeper understanding of Stoic philosophy, its application, and its enduring relevance. His philosophy and its impact underline the universality and timelessness of Stoic wisdom.

Epictetus's teaching on the dichotomy of control offers a fresh perspective on dealing with life's ups and downs. This simple but profound idea encourages us to distinguish between what we can control and what we can't, and to focus our energy only on the former. It's a liberating principle that can free us from unnecessary stress and anxiety. In a world where we often feel compelled to control everything, this Stoic lesson is a welcome reminder that certain things are beyond our control, and that's perfectly fine.

Consider his statement: "Freedom is the only worthy goal in life. It is won by disregarding things that lie beyond our control." This quote speaks to the Stoic pursuit of freedom, but not in the physical sense—Epictetus himself lived much of his life as a slave. Instead, it speaks to inner freedom, the ability to maintain peace of mind and calmness of spirit regardless of external circumstances. This is a powerful lesson for us all, reminding us that while we may not be able to control everything that happens to us, we can control our response.

Epictetus's ideas also offer invaluable insights into the nature of human relationships. His teachings remind us of the importance of empathy, understanding, and accepting others. In his Discourses, Epictetus advised: "When you see someone weeping in grief...don't hesitate to sympathize with him or even...join in his lamentations. But take care that you don't lament internally, too." This quote embodies the Stoic perspective on empathy—it's essential to connect with and support others in their pain but equally important to maintain your own emotional balance.

Personally, I've found Epictetus's teachings to be a reliable guide in my journey towards understanding Stoicism. His lessons on control, freedom, and empathy have not only provided theoretical knowledge but also practical tools to apply Stoic principles in my daily life. By internalizing his teachings, I've been able to cultivate inner peace, emotional resilience, and deeper connections with others.

In today's turbulent times, where change is the only constant, and uncertainty is an unavoidable part of life, Epictetus's teachings hold significant relevance. His timeless wisdom can guide us to lead more fulfilling lives, fostering resilience, tranquility, and a greater sense of control. By understanding and interpreting his teachings, we gain an insight into the heart of Stoic philosophy and its practical utility in our lives. This exploration underscores the enduring impact of Epictetus's philosophy and the timeless wisdom it embodies.

THE LEGACY OF EPICTETUS

The legacy of Epictetus extends far beyond his time, continuing to resonate with audiences millennia after his death. His teachings are not merely historical artefacts but practical tools that still hold great relevance in our modern society. He remains one of the most influential figures in Stoic philosophy, his thoughts persistently guiding individuals in their pursuit of a virtuous and fulfilling life.

Epictetus's distinctive emphasis on inner freedom and control continues to be a cornerstone in modern self-help and personal development literature. His Dichotomy of Control is frequently employed in cognitive-behavioral therapy, where it aids individuals in distinguishing between what they can and cannot change, thereby reducing anxiety and increasing resilience. In the world of business and leadership, Epictetus's teachings on stoicism provide a framework for decision-making, emphasizing calmness, clarity, and the courage to accept reality as it is.

Furthermore, Epictetus's influence isn't confined to academic or professional settings; his wisdom permeates various aspects of our everyday lives. From dealing with personal setbacks to nurturing relationships, his principles provide a compass for navigating the complexities of life. His notion of inner freedom, his teaching that happiness depends not on external events but on our responses to them, has helped countless individuals find contentment in their lives, regardless of their circumstances.

In addition to his practical teachings, Epictetus has also left a lasting impact on philosophical discourse. He played a crucial role in shaping the Stoic school of thought, and his writings remain foundational texts in the study of Stoicism. He has inspired philosophers, writers, and thinkers throughout history, including the Roman Emperor Marcus Aurelius, who was deeply influenced by his teachings.

Finally, Epictetus's legacy lies in the transformative power of his teachings. For those who delve into his work and internalize his philosophy, life takes on a new light. Challenges become opportunities for growth, relationships become arenas for practicing virtue, and personal freedom becomes an achievable goal.

In conclusion, Epictetus's enduring legacy is a testament to the profound wisdom and practical value of his teachings. His philosophy continues to inspire, influence, and guide individuals across the globe, ensuring his place in history as a pivotal figure in Stoic philosophy and one of humanity's most influential thinkers.

———

The journey through Epictetus's life and teachings has been an enlightening exploration of the practical applications and transformative power of Stoicism. Despite his humble beginnings and the adversity he faced, Epictetus embodies the very essence of Stoicism: the pursuit of virtue and wisdom, and the recognition that while we cannot control everything that happens to us, we can control how we respond. This foundational principle, embedded within all of Epictetus's teachings, still speaks to us with striking relevance today.

Epictetus's profound influence extends beyond his immediate context to shape the development of Stoic philosophy and its interpretation by later generations. His teachings are not just historical relics but living wisdom, continually guiding those seeking peace and fulfillment amidst life's uncertainties and challenges.

As we conclude this chapter, we carry forward the insights and inspiration derived from Epictetus's teachings. We take with us the understanding that Stoicism is not a static doctrine, but a vibrant philosophy that adapts to our evolving individual and collective experiences.

In the next chapter, we start our journey with Epictetus, a man who rose from slavery to become one of the most influential Stoic philosophers. His life and teachings continue to inspire millions of people around the world, including myself. I invite you to join me as we delve into his world and explore his wisdom.

CHAPTER 7
MARCUS AURELIUS - A STOIC EMPEROR

Marcus Aurelius, the embodiment of the philosopher-king, straddled the worlds of imperial power and contemplative wisdom with a dignity and resilience that still echo through the millennia. Born in 121 AD, he reigned as the Roman Emperor from 161 to 180 AD. His rule marked the end of a period referred to by historians as the Pax Romana, an era of relative peace and stability for the Empire. However, it is not merely his political legacy that has immortalized Marcus Aurelius; it is his profound contributions to philosophy that truly define his enduring influence.

The Stoic Emperor, as he is often referred to, was the personification of the Stoic ideal, that philosophy should not merely be a subject of intellectual debate, but rather a way of life. His dedication to Stoic principles didn't merely inform his reign but pervaded his personal life, offering us a clear vision of how these principles can be lived out, not just theorized.

The Stoic philosophy, dating back to the 3rd century BC, is known for its focus on virtue, duty, and acceptance, preaching the cultivation of an unshakeable peace of mind and the mastery over one's emotions. It divides things into those we control—our mind and actions—and those we cannot—the external world. Marcus Aurelius, despite being one of the most powerful men on earth, demonstrated this division through his life, showing the world how to focus on controlling the self rather than futilely attempting to control the world.

Marcus Aurelius's most significant contribution to Stoicism, and indeed the world, is his personal journal, now known as the "Meditations". These writings, intended for personal reflection rather than public view, offer an intimate look into his thoughts and struggles. They reflect his persistent pursuit of virtue and wisdom in a world fraught with power, warfare, and adversity. Today, the Meditations serve as one of the most profound and influential works in Stoic literature, continuing to provide guidance and solace to millions worldwide.

In the figure of Marcus Aurelius, we are offered a unique insight into the practical application of Stoic principles. He was not just a philosopher in a palace but an emperor in a tumultuous world, leading an empire through wars and plagues, guided by Stoic principles. In the following sections, we will delve deeper into his life, his Stoic philosophy, and how it has influenced the generations that followed.

EARLY LIFE AND PATH TO STOICISM

Marcus Aurelius was born on April 26, 121 AD, in Rome, to a prominent and politically active family. His family lineage was one of significance, with a long history of public service, and this pedigree paved the way for Marcus's future as a leader. However, even as a young boy, it became evident that Marcus was not simply destined to follow the beaten path of his ancestors; he was destined to carve his own.

Marcus's early life was not without its unique trials. His father passed away when he was just three, leaving him in the care of his grandfather. Despite the loss, his upbringing was far from neglected. He was bestowed with an exemplary education and cultivated in an environment of affluence and intellect. A testament to his grandfather's dedication to his education was the assembly of eminent tutors assigned to him. This illustrious group included the acclaimed rhetoric tutor Marcus Cornelius Fronto and the respected Stoic philosopher Quintus Junius Rusticus.

The figure of Quintus Junius Rusticus was particularly influential in Marcus's philosophical development. Rusticus was a renowned Stoic philosopher and, importantly, a man of action, serving as the urban prefect of Rome. Rusticus is often credited with introducing Marcus to the philosophy of Stoicism, a move that profoundly shaped Marcus's world view and ignited a lifelong passion for Stoic thought. Rusticus offered him his own copy of the teachings of Epictetus, a former slave turned Stoic philosopher, which served as the gateway into Stoic philosophy for Marcus.

Marcus's deepening interest in philosophy was considered unusual for someone of his status. In an era when the young nobility were primarily engrossed in the pursuit of pleasure and the political game, Marcus displayed a remarkable thirst for wisdom and understanding. At a young age, he began to wear the traditional attire of a Greek philosopher, the rough cloak, and slept on the ground, much to the worry of his mother and tutors. But for Marcus, this was not merely an affectation; it was a deliberate and profound commitment to the principles and practices of Stoicism.

The decision to adopt Stoicism was not an easy path, especially for someone who was thrust into a life of political power and responsibility. Stoicism required one to focus on personal virtue, control over one's emotions, and acceptance of fate – principles that often seemed at odds with the harsh realities of political leadership. However, Marcus was undeterred. Despite the challenges, he dedicated himself wholeheartedly to the practice of Stoicism, allowing its principles to guide his actions and decisions. This commitment to Stoic philosophy was not only a testament to his strength of character but also a testament to the practicality and robustness of Stoic principles.

As we delve further into Marcus's life and philosophy, we can glean insights into how Stoicism helped him navigate not only his personal struggles but also the trials and tribulations he faced as an emperor. His path to Stoicism was one of personal growth and self-transformation, a journey that would profoundly shape the course of his life and his reign as the Emperor of Rome. Marcus's early life and his journey to Stoicism serve as a potent reminder of the transformative power of philosophy, not just as an intellectual exercise but as a guide to living a fulfilling and meaningful life.

The events and experiences of Marcus's early life were instrumental in laying the foundation for his Stoic journey. These elements of his upbringing were crucial in shaping his character, honing his intellect, and fostering a keen sense of duty and responsibility. Stoicism, with its emphasis on virtue, self-control, and acceptance of fate, resonated deeply with Marcus. It offered a framework through which he could make sense of the world around him and his place within it.

Marcus's early encounters with Stoicism were marked by an earnest and sincere engagement with its principles. This was not a mere academic interest for him; Stoicism was a way of life. He absorbed the teachings of the Stoic philosophers and actively sought to incorporate their wisdom into his daily life. His actions and choices were guided by Stoic principles, reflecting a deep commitment to the philosophy that extended beyond the intellectual realm.

However, the journey to Stoicism was not always smooth for Marcus. He grappled with the inherent tensions between the Stoic ideals and the demands of his role as a future emperor. Stoicism, with its emphasis on tranquility, introspection, and independence from external circumstances, was seemingly at odds with the tumultuous world of politics, marked by power struggles, diplomatic challenges, and the weight of public responsibility. Yet, Marcus remained steadfast in his commitment to Stoic philosophy. His determination to reconcile his philosophical convictions with his political duties underscored his dedication to Stoicism.

This period of Marcus's life, marked by personal growth and philosophical exploration, culminated in his full acceptance of Stoic philosophy. This was a transformative period for him, as he evolved from a student of Stoicism to a practitioner. Marcus's transition to Stoicism was not an abrupt shift; instead, it was a gradual process that reflected his thoughtful engagement with the philosophy. It was during these formative years that Marcus began to crystallize his understanding of Stoic principles and integrate them into his life.

The path to Stoicism shaped Marcus Aurelius in profound ways, and his journey offers valuable insights into the transformative potential of Stoicism. His life serves as a powerful example of how Stoicism, when sincerely and thoughtfully practiced, can offer a compelling framework for personal growth, ethical living, and resilient leadership. As we delve deeper into Marcus's life, we will see how these Stoic principles guided his decisions, shaped his reign, and contributed to his legacy as a Stoic emperor.

MARCUS AURELIUS AS EMPEROR

Ascending the throne in 161 AD, Marcus Aurelius assumed the role of Emperor of the Roman Empire, a position that carried immense power and responsibility. Here, Marcus was tasked with managing vast territories, handling delicate diplomatic relations, quelling internal strife, and leading military campaigns. Each of these tasks brought its unique set of challenges, yet Marcus was determined to handle them with the wisdom and temperance that Stoicism promoted.

Marcus's reign was a unique blend of philosophy and pragmatism, where the philosophical principles of Stoicism were applied in practical decision-making. Stoicism was not just a theoretical framework for Marcus; it was a guide to action, a compass that directed his decisions, and a source of strength in trying times.

The reign of Marcus Aurelius was fraught with challenges. His rule was marked by wars on several fronts, political intrigue, economic instability, and a deadly plague that swept across the empire. Despite these adversities, Marcus remained resolute and anchored in his Stoic principles. His approach to these challenges reflected the core tenets of Stoicism: accepting what he could not change, focusing on his actions which were within his control, and maintaining tranquility of mind amid the chaos.

Marcus's Stoic philosophy provided him with a unique perspective on power. Instead of being intoxicated by his authority, Marcus used it as a tool to promote justice, harmony, and the wellbeing of his people. His power was not an end in itself, but a means to the greater end of serving the common good.

Moreover, the Stoic ideal of virtue, which Marcus held in high regard, permeated his governance. His policies and reforms were guided by a sense of duty and the pursuit of the greater good, and he consistently placed the welfare of his people above personal gain or ambition. Marcus was known for his just rule, his respect for the Senate, and his commitment to improving the lives of the Roman people. His leadership style embodied the Stoic principle of serving others and contributing to the welfare of the community.

Throughout his reign, Marcus Aurelius demonstrated the viability and value of Stoic philosophy in real-world governance. His dedication to Stoicism was not merely theoretical; it was profoundly practical. Marcus was deeply committed to implementing Stoic principles in his rule, and he sought to align his actions with Stoic ideals of virtue, wisdom, and integrity.

Despite the adversities he faced, Marcus Aurelius remained steadfast in his Stoic principles. He faced each challenge with resilience and fortitude, viewing them not as obstacles but as opportunities for growth and learning. This approach to adversity, deeply rooted in Stoicism, contributed significantly to his effective leadership.

In conclusion, Marcus Aurelius's reign as emperor demonstrated the power and relevance of Stoicism in the realm of governance and leadership. He showed that it was possible to wield power while remaining true to Stoic ideals, and his leadership style offers a compelling model for those who aspire to lead with wisdom, virtue, and resilience.

Marcus's reign was undoubtedly shaped by his commitment to Stoicism. It guided his actions, informed his decisions, and helped him navigate the challenges of leadership. Through his example, we see the profound impact that Stoicism can have on a person's life and the world around them. Marcus Aurelius, the philosopher-emperor, remains an enduring testament to the power and practicality of Stoic philosophy.

MARCUS AURELIUS'S PHILOSOPHY AND ITS IMPACT

Marcus Aurelius's philosophical legacy is preserved largely through his personal journal, known today as the 'Meditations.' This collection of thoughts, written mostly during his military campaigns, is a profound repository of Stoic wisdom that continues to inspire and enlighten readers worldwide. In this section, we delve into some of his most influential quotes and teachings, seeking to understand their significance and relevance in both historical and contemporary contexts.

One of the most powerful quotes from Marcus Aurelius is: "You have power over your mind - not outside events. Realize this, and you will find strength." This is a cornerstone of Stoic philosophy, emphasizing the duality of control: we cannot control external events, but we can control our reactions to them.

The first part of the quote underscores our dominion over our own mind. This is a profound realization, often overlooked in our pursuit to shape the world around us. We spend countless hours trying to influence external circumstances, only to find that many factors are beyond our grasp. Marcus, however, urges us to redirect this effort inward. By focusing on our minds, which are within our control, we can develop resilience, wisdom, and inner peace.

The second part of the quote is a call to action. Once we realize and accept our limited sphere of control, we don't become passive or resigned. Instead, we discover a new kind of strength, a strength that arises from the acceptance of reality. This realization liberates us from the futile struggle of trying to control the uncontrollable, allowing us to focus our energy on what truly matters - our thoughts, attitudes, and actions.

In my own life, this quote has been transformative. Like many of us, I have often grappled with situations beyond my control, whether it's a delayed flight, a critical remark, or a global crisis. Initially, these circumstances would trigger stress, frustration, or worry. However, through Marcus's wisdom, I've learned to shift my focus from the uncontrollable to the controllable - my reaction to the situation.

Now, when confronted with a situation beyond my control, I strive to stay composed and find a positive angle or a lesson in the situation. This reframing doesn't make the problem disappear, but it does offer me the strength to face it with grace, patience, and wisdom. This quote has taught me that while we can't always control the storm, we can adjust our sails, and therein lies our true power.

Another of Marcus's impactful teachings is: "The happiness of your life depends upon the quality of your thoughts." This is a potent reminder of the power of our thoughts in shaping our lives. Often, we tend to attribute our happiness or unhappiness to external circumstances, overlooking the impact of our own thought processes. Marcus Aurelius challenges this perspective, advocating that our wellbeing is fundamentally tied to the quality of our thoughts.

From a historical standpoint, this teaching resonates deeply with Stoic philosophy's core tenets. The Stoics believed that our reactions, not events themselves, determine our peace of mind. They urged individuals to cultivate wisdom, virtue, and rational thinking, understanding that these internal qualities profoundly affect our experience of life.

In the contemporary context, Marcus's teaching aligns with modern psychological research, which increasingly recognizes the crucial role our thoughts play in shaping our emotions, behaviors, and overall well-being. Today, therapies like Cognitive Behavioral Therapy (CBT) echo Marcus's wisdom, helping individuals reshape their thoughts to improve their mental health.

In my personal journey with Stoicism, this teaching has been pivotal. I've come to realize that by nurturing positive, rational, and empathetic thoughts, I can significantly enhance my life's quality. This has not been an overnight transformation but a gradual process of introspection, self-awareness, and mental conditioning.

In essence, the philosophical legacy of Marcus Aurelius extends beyond the historical and cultural confines of the Roman Empire. His wisdom, captured in his quotes and teachings, offers timeless insights into the human condition. His teachings remind us of our power over our thoughts, the importance of focusing on what we can control, and the role our thought processes play in shaping our lives. These lessons have profoundly influenced my understanding of Stoicism and continue to guide me in my daily life.

Lastly, Marcus's philosophy impacts not only our individual lives but also our collective existence. His emphasis on virtue, justice, and the common good serves as a guiding light in our social interactions and communal responsibilities. His wisdom prompts us to reflect on our role in the larger social fabric and encourages us to strive for a more just, empathetic, and harmonious society.

Thus, the philosophical insights of Marcus Aurelius, echoing across centuries, still hold profound relevance. They invite us to cultivate resilience, wisdom, and virtue, fostering personal growth and contributing to societal betterment. Marcus's philosophy is not merely a historical artifact; it's a living, breathing source of inspiration that continues to illuminate our path in the quest for a fulfilling and meaningful life.

THE LEGACY OF MARCUS AURELIUS

The legacy of Marcus Aurelius has extended far beyond the boundaries of his reign and the ancient world. His Meditations have served as a perennial source of wisdom and guidance for countless individuals throughout history, shaping our understanding and practice of Stoicism and providing a blueprint for leading a virtuous and meaningful life.

Marcus Aurelius has often been recognized as a 'philosopher king,' an epithet that testifies to the unique synthesis of power and wisdom in his persona. He demonstrated to the world that it's possible to be a ruler without losing touch with one's moral compass, providing a template for effective, ethical leadership that's still pertinent today. His reign, marked by his commitment to justice, compassion, and duty, is a powerful illustration of Stoic principles put into action.

His teachings, notably those captured in Meditations, continue to resonate powerfully in the present day. This is particularly evident in the field of psychology, where many of Marcus's insights find a striking resemblance with modern therapeutic techniques. For instance, his philosophy echoes in the principles of Cognitive Behavioural Therapy (CBT), which teaches individuals to manage their problems by changing the way they think and behave, highlighting the profound influence of Marcus Aurelius on contemporary thought.

On a more personal level, his reflections on resilience in the face of adversity, equanimity amidst change, and the cultivation of virtue as the highest good offer invaluable guidance for navigating the challenges of modern life. His teachings serve as a reminder that while we may not control the world around us, we have the power to control our responses to it, empowering us to lead more fulfilled and purposeful lives.

Furthermore, the philosophy of Marcus Aurelius is not limited to personal self-improvement but extends to shaping a better society. His emphasis on the interconnectedness of all beings and the pursuit of the common good encourages us to strive for social harmony and justice, reinforcing the continuing relevance of his teachings in our collective consciousness.

The enduring legacy of Marcus Aurelius lies in his timeless wisdom, a testament to the power of Stoic philosophy in guiding human thought and action. His teachings, bridging the gap between antiquity and modernity, continue to inspire us, inviting us to pursue virtue, cultivate resilience, and contribute to the common good. His life, marked by a unique confluence of philosophical wisdom and practical leadership, serves as a beacon for all of us in our quest for a meaningful life. It's through this ongoing influence on individuals and societies that the legacy of Marcus Aurelius continues to thrive, rendering him a luminary not only of his era but of all time.

———

As we draw the chapter to a close, it becomes increasingly clear that Marcus Aurelius was more than just an emperor or a philosopher; he was a torchbearer of Stoicism, illuminating the path for others with his wisdom and conduct. His life and teachings offer invaluable insights into understanding and practicing Stoic philosophy, guiding us in our pursuit of wisdom, virtue, and tranquility.

His words resonate as deeply today as they did during his reign, reminding us of the enduring relevance of Stoicism. They encourage us to focus on what's within our control, cultivate resilience amidst adversities, and strive for virtue in all our actions. Marcus Aurelius's life serves as a powerful testament to the transformative potential of Stoic philosophy, providing inspiration and guidance for our journey.

As we move forward to explore the lives and teachings of other Stoic philosophers in subsequent chapters, Marcus Aurelius's influence remains indelible. His legacy continues to guide us, enriching our understanding of Stoicism and its profound impact on human life.

Let his wisdom infuse our journey ahead, as we delve deeper into the world of Stoicism, learning from the teachings of other great minds that have shaped this enduring philosophy. Marcus Aurelius's imprint on Stoicism sets a strong foundation, equipping us with the lens to discern and appreciate the profundity of Stoic philosophy that we will continue to explore.

In the next chapter, we'll delve into the life and teachings of another influential Stoic philosopher, Seneca, and continue our exploration of Stoicism's enduring relevance and impact.

CHAPTER 8
SENECA - THE STATESMAN AND PHILOSOPHER

eneca, or as he's formally known, Lucius Annaeus Seneca, is a name that's become synonymous with the later development of Stoic philosophy. Born in Corduba in the Roman province of Hispania, modern-day Spain, around the start of the Common Era, Seneca was more than a philosopher. He was a statesman, a dramatist, and one of the wealthiest and most powerful figures in Rome, a testament to his unique ability to merge thought with action in the true spirit of Stoicism.

As a philosopher, Seneca stands out for his practical approach to Stoicism. Rather than treat it as a detached theoretical discipline, he sought to weave it into the fabric of daily life, making it a practical guide for living virtuously and happily amidst the uncertainties and adversities of life. His works, such as "Letters from a Stoic" and "On the Shortness of Life," remain widely read and studied, bearing testament to the timeless appeal of his philosophy.

In his role as a statesman, Seneca served as an advisor to the Roman Emperor Nero, a position fraught with peril given Nero's notorious unpredictability. Despite the inherent risks, Seneca managed to use his position to effect some measure of good, steering Nero towards just decisions—at least in the early years of Nero's reign. His experiences in the political arena, coupled with his personal hardships, provided fertile ground for his exploration of Stoic philosophy.

As a dramatist, Seneca was one of the most significant contributors to Roman tragedy. His plays dealt with intense emotions, moral dilemmas, and the tragic repercussions of unbridled passion—themes that dovetailed with his Stoic views on emotional regulation and moral rectitude.

Seneca's ability to navigate the turbulent waters of Roman politics, his penetrating insights into the human condition, and his unwavering commitment to the Stoic path despite the vicissitudes of life make him a compelling figure in the annals of philosophy. His life and works offer valuable lessons on the application of Stoicism in the face of real-world challenges and serve as a testament to the transformative power of philosophy when applied to daily life. This chapter delves into the life, philosophy, and legacy of Seneca, illuminating the richness and relevance of his contribution to Stoicism.

Lucius Annaeus Seneca was born into a wealthy family in Corduba, Hispania, around 4 BC. His father, Seneca the Elder, was a famous rhetorician, and his mother, Helvia, came from a prominent family. Seneca was the second of three sons, and his family moved to Rome when he was still a child.

As was common for young men of his class, Seneca received an extensive education in rhetoric and philosophy, studying under some of the most renowned teachers of his time. These studies left a profound impression on young Seneca and sparked his lifelong interest in philosophy. His early education was heavily influenced by Stoic philosophy, which promoted the virtues of wisdom, justice, courage, and temperance.

However, Seneca's life wasn't all scholarly pursuits. In his early twenties, he battled serious health problems. He suffered from respiratory issues, possibly tuberculosis, which caused him significant distress and pain. Yet, it was in the crucible of this suffering that Seneca found solace in Stoicism. He found in Stoicism the mental tools to cope with his physical discomfort and the uncertainty of life. As he once wrote, "He who has made a fair compact with poverty is rich."

Seneca's career as a statesman began under the reign of Emperor

Claudius. He was first appointed quaestor, an initial step in the political ladder in Rome, and later became a senator. However, his political career was fraught with difficulties. He was exiled to Corsica by Claudius's wife, Agrippina the Younger, on charges of adultery with Julia Livilla, the sister of Caligula.

Seneca's exile lasted for eight years, during which he devoted himself to philosophy and writing. In his writings from this period, we see a man trying to make sense of his circumstances and maintain his equanimity amidst adversity. Stoicism wasn't just an abstract theory for Seneca; it was a way of life that helped him endure hardship with fortitude.

Agrippina eventually recalled Seneca from exile to tutor her son, Nero, who would later become emperor. As Nero's advisor, Seneca was tasked with shaping the young man's character and instilling in him the values of Stoicism. Despite the many challenges and moral dilemmas he faced in this role, Seneca remained committed to his Stoic principles.

In sum, Seneca's path to Stoicism was marked by personal hardship, political intrigue, and moral challenges. It was a journey that tested his commitment to Stoic principles and ultimately solidified his reputation as one of the most influential Stoic philosophers. His life serves as a testament to the transformative power of Stoicism, not only as a philosophy but as a practical guide to living well amidst life's challenges.

However, despite his Stoic leanings, Seneca was not without his contradictions. As a wealthy senator and advisor to the emperor, Seneca had amassed a considerable fortune. This was in stark contrast to the Stoic teachings which prioritized virtue over material wealth. These contradictions in his life caused many to question the authenticity of his commitment to Stoic philosophy. Still, Seneca defended himself, arguing that it was not wealth that was problematic but the unhealthy attachment to it.

While in service of Nero, Seneca found himself in a precarious situation. His student, once seen as a promising young leader, increasingly became erratic and tyrannical. Seneca was often caught in the middle, trying to mitigate Nero's worst impulses while attempting to uphold his own philosophical principles.

In 65 AD, Seneca was accused of conspiring in the Pisonian conspiracy to assassinate Nero. Although there's no clear historical evidence of his involvement, he was ordered by Nero to commit suicide. Seneca accepted his fate with Stoic composure. His death, like his life, was a testament to his commitment to Stoic principles.

Seneca's path to Stoicism wasn't straightforward. It was marked by both personal and political turbulence. However, through all his trials and tribulations, Seneca found in Stoicism a guiding philosophy. His writings remain as a testament to his efforts to understand, interpret, and live by Stoic principles, thus offering a window into the thoughts and struggles of one of Stoicism's most prolific and complex figures.

In many ways, Seneca embodies the very essence of Stoicism. Despite his wealth and political power, he grappled with the same existential questions that each of us faces: How should we live? What do we value? How do we cope with adversity? His writings, marked by his unique blend of philosophical reflection and practical advice, continue to provide guidance and solace to many, making Seneca a critical figure in the Stoic tradition.

SENECA'S CAREER AND CHALLENGES

Lucius Annaeus Seneca, also known as Seneca the Younger, held a prominent position in Roman society, navigating through an array of political challenges and personal tragedies that would leave a lasting impact on his philosophical writings. Born into an equestrian family in Cordoba, Spain, in 4 BC, he was brought to Rome during his infancy. From an early age, he was introduced to Stoic philosophy, which would later prove instrumental in guiding him through the tumultuous turns his life would take.

As a senator and advisor to Emperor Nero, Seneca held significant influence in Rome. He was not just a philosopher in the abstract; his philosophies were tested in the real world of political intrigue, power, and corruption. His political career reached its zenith when he became the tutor and then the advisor to Nero, the young and then still promising emperor.

However, this prominent position was not without its perils. He was accused of adultery with Julia Livilla, the sister of Emperor Caligula, leading to his banishment to Corsica in 41 AD. Despite this setback, Seneca adhered to his Stoic beliefs. He accepted the exile with composure, using this time for reflection and writing. His stoicism during this period is captured in his writing, "Consolation to Helvia", a letter to his mother expressing his philosophical reflections on his exile. He wrote, "I am not so much grieved that I am now away, as joyful that I once was with you. When one takes pleasure in recalling his hardships, they are then truly ended."

His return to Rome in 49 AD came with the adoption of Agrippina's son, Nero, by Claudius. It was a tumultuous time in Roman history, marked by political intrigues and power struggles. As Nero's tutor and later advisor, Seneca tried to temper Nero's worst impulses with philosophical wisdom, but his efforts ultimately proved futile. Despite being one of Rome's most influential men, Seneca could not control the escalating tyranny of Nero, eventually falling out of favor.

Seneca's personal life was also marked by tragedies and hardships. He suffered from poor health, including bouts of asthma that often brought him near to death. He witnessed the decline of Rome under Nero's rule and ultimately was ordered to commit suicide by Nero himself, accused of involvement in the Pisonian conspiracy. In all these instances, his commitment to Stoicism offered him a perspective to accept life's vicissitudes calmly. His ability to remain resolute and composed in the face of adversity stands as a testament to his philosophical beliefs.

In the next part, we will delve deeper into Seneca's philosophy and teachings, dissecting the ways in which they continue to resonate and provide guidance in the modern world.

It's essential to understand the circumstances that enveloped Seneca's life to fully appreciate his commitment to Stoicism. He was known for his oratorical skills, which made him a prominent figure in Nero's court. However, Seneca's reputation was often tarnished by accusations of hypocrisy, primarily because his immense wealth seemed to contradict the Stoic ideal of living a simple and unencumbered life. Seneca himself acknowledged this contradiction in his letters, offering a nuanced perspective on wealth from a Stoic viewpoint. He argued that wealth in itself is not a vice; rather, it becomes problematic when it controls us, distracts us from virtue, or is acquired unjustly.

Seneca's contributions to literature and drama were significant and highly recognized in his time. He was one of Rome's leading playwrights, with his tragedies deeply reflecting Stoic ideas. These works focused on the emotional struggles of their characters, portraying intense passions as destructive forces. In his view, these passions could only be tamed by reason – a key tenet of Stoic philosophy.

Despite his illustrious career, Seneca was not exempt from the harsh realities of life. He faced exile, suffered from debilitating health issues, and lived under constant threat due to his proximity to the volatile emperor Nero. These adversities only strengthened his resolve to live according to Stoic principles.

After being implicated in the Pisonian conspiracy, a plot against Nero, Seneca was ordered to commit suicide, a common sentence for the Roman aristocracy involved in political scandals. The accounts of his death reflect the bravery and equanimity he had professed in his philosophical writings. Seneca took his own life in a manner consistent with the teachings of Stoicism, showcasing his steadfast adherence to his philosophy even in the face of death.

Seneca's life and career, marked by both remarkable achievements and profound challenges, offer a testament to the resilience of the human spirit and the power of Stoic philosophy. He navigated through the volatile landscape of Roman politics, personal tragedies, and health issues, always returning to the Stoic principles of courage, wisdom, justice, and temperance.

Through his writings, Seneca offered guidance on how to face adversity with grace and courage. Despite the passage of time, his insights remain as relevant as ever, providing guidance and comfort to anyone navigating through life's inevitable challenges. His teachings not only shed light on Stoic philosophy but also inspire us to live with resilience, purpose, and equanimity, demonstrating the timeless appeal of Stoicism.

SENECA'S PHILOSOPHY AND ITS IMPACT

Seneca's philosophy centered on the principles of Stoicism, but he was also deeply influenced by other philosophical schools. This eclectic approach allowed him to tailor his Stoic teachings, making them more approachable and applicable to the everyday life of his contemporaries. Unlike the more theoretical approach adopted by other Stoic philosophers, Seneca emphasized the practical application of Stoic principles. His letters and essays are filled with advice on dealing with anger, fear, grief, and other emotions that, according to Stoicism, disturb our peace of mind.

One of Seneca's most significant contributions to Stoicism is his discourse on the proper use of time, which he explored in his essay, "On the Shortness of Life." Here, he argued that life is long enough if we use our time wisely, focusing on what truly matters and letting go of trivial concerns. This teaching continues to resonate in our modern world, often characterized by constant busyness and distraction.

Seneca's philosophical teachings, filled with practical wisdom and acute observations about human nature, have greatly influenced Western thought. His writings have been studied and admired by great thinkers throughout history, from early Christian theologians to Enlightenment philosophers. His thoughts on subjects like power, wealth, and morality have shaped ethical and political theories, contributing to the intellectual heritage of the West.

Furthermore, Seneca's teachings have had a profound influence on the development of modern cognitive therapies. His advice on managing destructive emotions echoes in cognitive-behavioral therapy (CBT), a widely used psychological treatment method. CBT practitioners often quote Seneca's philosophy, reinforcing the idea that it's not the events themselves that disturb us, but our perception of them.

Personally, delving into Seneca's philosophy has been an enlightening journey. His practical wisdom, his insightful observations about human nature, and his unwavering commitment to Stoic principles have deeply influenced my understanding of Stoicism. His teachings have served as a guide for navigating life's challenges, encouraging a mindful and virtuous approach to living.

One of Seneca's quotes that deeply resonate with me is, "We suffer more often in imagination than in reality." This simple yet profound statement reminds us of the power of our thoughts and the importance of maintaining a rational perspective. Instead of getting carried away by our fears and anxieties, we should take a step back, analyze our thoughts, and challenge any irrational beliefs. This principle, a key tenet of Stoic philosophy and cognitive therapy alike, is an effective strategy for managing stress and achieving peace of mind.

In another notable teaching, Seneca advises us to prepare ourselves for future adversities: "He who has prepared the mind in advance for the coming of evils has conquered them already." This perspective encourages us to develop resilience, reminding us that challenges are an inevitable part of life. By mentally preparing for adversity, we can lessen its impact and maintain our composure even in tough times. This principle has greatly influenced my approach to life, instilling a sense of resilience and equanimity.

Moreover, Seneca's emphasis on the value of time resonates profoundly with me. In our fast-paced, distraction-filled world, his wisdom serves as a reminder to use our time wisely and focus on what truly matters. His teachings have helped me realize the importance of living fully in the present, appreciating the beauty of each moment, and prioritizing meaningful pursuits over trivial concerns.

By distilling complex philosophical concepts into practical advice, Seneca's teachings offer valuable insights for managing life's challenges and pursuing a virtuous life. His philosophy serves as a guide for cultivating resilience, tranquility, and wisdom – key principles of Stoic philosophy that continue to be relevant in our modern world.

In conclusion, Seneca's philosophy provides a rich source of wisdom for understanding Stoicism and navigating life's challenges. His teachings, which strike a balance between theoretical concepts and practical advice, continue to resonate with readers around the world, shaping our understanding of Stoic philosophy and its relevance to our lives. Whether we're dealing with personal struggles, professional challenges, or existential questions, Seneca's philosophy offers timeless insights for achieving peace of mind and living a virtuous life.

THE LEGACY OF SENECA

Despite the passing of almost two millennia, the legacy of Seneca endures. His wisdom continues to enlighten and inspire individuals to lead virtuous and fulfilled lives. Seneca's letters, essays, and tragedies are still widely read and analyzed, offering insights into the Stoic philosophy and the human condition.

Through his writings, Seneca has left us with a comprehensive view of Stoicism in practice. He taught us that philosophy is not merely a subject for academic study but a guide for life. His teachings emphasize that one's character and virtue are the most significant factors in achieving a good life.

Beyond his philosophical writings, Seneca's life story also provides valuable lessons. Despite his many trials and tribulations, he demonstrated resilience and commitment to his principles, embodying the Stoic ideal of equanimity in the face of adversity. Even in his final moments, he showed courage and tranquility, serving as an enduring example of Stoic wisdom in action.

In the realm of politics and drama, Seneca's influence is also evident. His critiques of tyranny and exploration of moral issues in his plays have continued to resonate in political and cultural discourse. His tragedies, imbued with Stoic philosophy, continue to be performed and adapted, attesting to their timeless appeal.

Furthermore, Seneca's teachings have found relevance in modern psychology. Concepts such as cognitive reframing and the control dichotomy closely align with techniques used in cognitive-behavioral therapy, demonstrating the enduring applicability of his wisdom.

In summary, Seneca's legacy is manifold. As a philosopher, his teachings provide a practical guide to leading a virtuous life. As a statesman and dramatist, his works continue to influence political and cultural discourses. His life story, marked by resilience and tranquility in the face of adversity, serves as an embodiment of Stoic principles. With his enduring wisdom, Seneca continues to guide us in navigating the complexities of life, solidifying his place in the annals of Stoic philosophy.

———

In reflecting on the life and teachings of Seneca, we gain a holistic understanding of Stoicism. Seneca's life, filled with its fair share of trials, triumphs, and tragedies, demonstrates Stoicism's practicality in the face of life's vicissitudes. His writings are not only filled with profound philosophical insight but also provide a practical guide for achieving tranquility and contentment in our daily lives.

Through Seneca, we learn that Stoicism is not a detached, intellectual exercise but a pragmatic philosophy that addresses real-life challenges. The Stoic principles he espoused, such as the control dichotomy, the pursuit of virtue, and the acceptance of fate, offer timeless wisdom that remains relevant in the modern world.

Seneca's enduring legacy testifies to the power and relevance of his teachings. Even as we transition into the next chapter, exploring another influential Stoic figure, we carry with us the lessons from Seneca. His life and teachings provide a rich tapestry of insights that enrich our understanding of Stoicism, continuing to guide us on our philosophical journey.

This concludes the chapter on Seneca, an eminent Stoic philosopher whose teachings continue to inspire and guide us to live virtuous and fulfilled lives. In the following chapter, we will delve into the life and philosophy of another significant Stoic figure, deepening our exploration of this transformative school of thought.

CHAPTER 9
ZENO OF CITIUM - THE FOUNDER OF STOICISM

Z eno of Citium, a man of resilience, introspection, and virtue, is a prominent figure in the realm of philosophy, widely acknowledged as the founder of Stoicism. Born in the city of Citium, on the island of Cyprus, around 334 BCE, he made an indelible mark on the course of philosophical thinking that continues to resonate in our contemporary world. Stoicism, a school of philosophy acclaimed for its practical applications, owes its inception to this distinguished thinker, whose life and teachings inspire the pursuit of wisdom, courage, justice, and temperance.

Zeno's journey to becoming a philosopher was far from typical. His early life as a successful merchant was abruptly interrupted by a shipwreck, a seeming catastrophe that inadvertently placed him on the path of philosophy. His journey, one that evolved from loss to enlightenment, uniquely situates Zeno among the pantheon of great philosophers and gives credence to the Stoic belief in facing adversity with equanimity.

As the founder of Stoicism, Zeno's impact cannot be understated. His teachings, brought to life through his books, such as "Republic", showcase the philosophical principles that form the bedrock of Stoicism. These principles focus on the cultivation of virtue, the acceptance of events beyond our control, and the importance of rationality in leading a fulfilling life.

The Stoic school, founded by Zeno in the stoa poikile (painted porch) in Athens, is where Stoicism derives its name. Zeno spent many years here, discussing philosophy with his followers and shaping the core tenets of Stoic thought. His philosophical teachings, centered around the idea that virtue is the highest good and that we should be indifferent to external events, set the precedent for later Stoic philosophers like Seneca, Epictetus, and Marcus Aurelius.

Despite the passing of centuries, Zeno's profound influence endures in the practice of Stoicism today. His foundational principles serve as a guide for many in leading a virtuous and fulfilling life, further cementing his role as a leading figure in Stoic philosophy. Zeno of Citium, thus, remains an embodiment of Stoic virtues, and his teachings continue to enlighten us on leading a life of wisdom and tranquility.

EARLY LIFE AND PATH TO STOICISM

Zeno of Citium, the founder of Stoicism, was born into a mercantile family around 334 BCE on the island of Cyprus. The island was renowned for its bustling ports, and maritime trade was the lifeblood of its economy. Zeno's early life was firmly rooted in this thriving mercantile environment, where he was primed to continue his family's trade business.

From an early age, Zeno was exposed to the intricate workings of commerce, the unpredictability of the sea, and the diverse cultures and philosophies that passed through the busy ports of Cyprus. This rich tapestry of experiences cultivated in him an inquisitive mind and resilience, characteristics that would later form the bedrock of his philosophical musings.

However, life had an unexpected twist in store for Zeno. On a voyage to Phoenicia, his ship met with a terrible storm and wrecked. Zeno found himself in Athens, a city considered the intellectual center of the world, bereft of his cargo but not his spirit. It was in this city, amid its storied streets and renowned schools of thought, that Zeno's philosophical journey began.

Guided by a bookseller, Zeno encountered a book by Socrates that profoundly influenced him. Impressed by the Socratic argument and intrigued by the discipline of philosophy, he sought guidance from the city's eminent philosophers. He studied under the Cynic philosopher Crates, the Megarian philosopher Stilpo, and the Platonist Xenocrates. From Crates, he learned the value of ascetic living, from Stilpo, the importance of logic, and from Xenocrates, the intricacies of metaphysics.

Yet, Zeno wasn't entirely satisfied with what he learned from these philosophers. He saw value in their teachings but felt that something was missing—a unified philosophy that could offer practical guidance for leading a virtuous life. And thus, Zeno set about developing his philosophy, drawing upon his diverse experiences as a merchant, a shipwreck survivor, and a student of philosophy. This culmination of experiences and teachings eventually led to the birth of Stoicism, a school of thought that emphasized living in accordance with nature, accepting things beyond our control, and focusing on self-improvement.

Zeno's journey to philosophy underscores the Stoic belief that every event, however adverse, can lead to something beneficial. In his case, a shipwreck led him to philosophy, where he found not just a means of understanding the world but also a practical guide for leading a fulfilling life. His unique path to philosophy thus serves as an inspiring testament to the power of resilience and the potential for personal growth amid adversity.

In Athens, Zeno spent years immersing himself in different philosophical schools, soaking up wisdom from learned minds. This was a transformative period for Zeno, who had been accustomed to a life driven by trade and commerce. The intellectual rigor of Athens shaped his perspective, making him realize the inherent instability of worldly possessions and the importance of cultivating inner virtues.

His experiences in the city's philosophical circles allowed him to observe the gaps in the prevalent philosophical doctrines. He noted how some schools focused on metaphysics but neglected practical ethics, while others espoused asceticism to the detriment of societal engagement. Zeno felt the need for a more balanced philosophy, one that could offer a holistic approach to life.

His pursuit for such a philosophy was not a hasty endeavor. Zeno was a patient man, a quality he had inherited from his life as a merchant, where hasty decisions could lead to disastrous outcomes. He spent two decades studying under different philosophers, gaining profound insights and honing his logical reasoning.

As he assimilated these philosophical teachings, Zeno maintained an open mind, welcoming constructive criticism and engaging in lively debates. This open-mindedness and patience, coupled with his innate resilience, guided him to develop Stoicism. It was a philosophy born out of lived experiences and critical engagement with diverse philosophical ideas, making it inherently practical and universally appealing.

Indeed, the circumstances of Zeno's early life and his journey to philosophy were far from ordinary. His transformation from a merchant to the founder of one of the most influential schools of philosophy is a story of resilience, patience, and relentless pursuit of knowledge. Zeno's life, much like his philosophy, exemplifies the potential of the human spirit to rise above adversity and seek wisdom. His journey serves as a powerful reminder of Stoicism's core principle: we cannot control external events, but we can control our responses to them.

ZENO'S PHILOSOPHICAL JOURNEY AND THE BIRTH OF STOICISM

Zeno's philosophical journey was far from linear. After the shipwreck that brought him to Athens, he immersed himself in the study of philosophy under Crates the Cynic. The Cynic School, founded by Antisthenes, a pupil of Socrates, proposed a radical idea - happiness could be obtained by rejecting all unnecessary desires and by living only for virtue. Zeno studied and adopted these principles but found the complete rejection of societal conventions and physical discomfort promoted by Cynicism extreme.

From the Megarian school, under the guidance of Stilpo, Zeno learned dialectics and logic, skills that would be crucial for the foundation of Stoicism. The Megarians were particularly known for their logic puzzles and wordplay, tools used to scrutinize ideas, beliefs, and arguments. Zeno's involvement with this school honed his intellectual rigor and ability to dissect and analyze philosophical arguments.

Zeno also spent time studying under the Platonists, followers of the renowned philosopher Plato. He was influenced by Plato's emphasis on the Forms - the abstract, perfect entities existing in a realm beyond the physical world. Although Zeno would ultimately disagree with the concept of an abstract realm separate from our physical reality, the Platonist idea that virtue equates with knowledge significantly influenced his ethical considerations.

After these enriching years of learning, Zeno felt ready to forge his own philosophical path. He combined elements of Cynicism, Megarian dialectic, and Platonism to form a new school of thought: Stoicism. This was a philosophy not born out of isolation but through a thoughtful combination of already existing philosophies, which he modified and fused together to fit his own observations and experiences.

The principles of Stoicism established by Zeno were grounded in the belief that virtue is the highest form of goodness and that it is sufficient for happiness. Virtue, in Stoic thought, corresponds to knowledge, and vice corresponds to ignorance. As such, the wise are virtuous and happy, and happiness and moral virtue are synonymous.

Zeno's Stoicism also emphasized the importance of accepting the natural order of things. In alignment with the logic he learned from the Megarians, Zeno taught that our world is an expression of a divine, rational order known as the Logos. Therefore, to live in accordance with nature, as Stoics strive to do, means to recognize and accept this divine order.

These principles reflected a break from the status quo, a philosophy that was practical, focused on personal ethics, and available to all, regardless of their societal status. Thus, Zeno of Citium established Stoicism, a philosophy designed for everyday life and one that would endure for centuries to come, influencing countless individuals on their journey towards achieving peace of mind and living virtuous lives.

ZENO'S TEACHINGS AND THEIR IMPACT

Zeno's impact on philosophy is not limited to the sphere of ethics. He made significant contributions to other areas, including logic and physics, which became important elements of Stoic philosophy. Zeno's view of logic, for instance, was innovative and instrumental in the development of Stoicism. He considered logic not just as a tool for argument but as a means to discern truth and steer clear of error. This focus on rationality, clarity, and precision is a defining characteristic of Stoic philosophy.

In terms of physics, Zeno postulated a pantheistic view of the universe, considering it a single, living entity where God is synonymous with nature. He believed in the rational structure of the universe, with everything happening out of necessity in accordance with the logos or universal reason. This belief had a significant influence on how Stoics perceive the world, leading them to accept things as they are and live in accordance with nature.

One cannot discuss Zeno's impact without mentioning the Stoic community he initiated, known as the Stoa Poikile or Painted Porch. This place became the epicenter of Stoic teaching and philosophy. Zeno's teachings were disseminated to a wide range of audiences, from ordinary citizens to influential figures of his time. The school continued to operate for almost 500 years, further testament to the enduring influence of Zeno's philosophical contributions.

In the modern world, Zeno's teachings continue to resonate. His emphasis on virtue as the only good and on accepting things we cannot control are lessons that seem particularly relevant today. In an era where we are often judged by material success and where many things seem outside of our control, the serenity and inner peace offered by Stoic philosophy is an attractive proposition for many. As the founder of Stoicism, Zeno's impact continues to be felt, not just in academic circles, but also in the lives of ordinary people seeking wisdom and tranquility.

ZENO'S PHILOSOPHICAL JOURNEY AND THE BIRTH OF STOICISM

Zeno of Citium, once an affluent merchant, found his life's purpose in philosophy. His journey into the intellectual realm was initiated by a catastrophic shipwreck that washed him onto the shores of Athens, a city known for its thriving philosophical scene. Unmoored from his previous life, Zeno was drawn into the rich intellectual tapestry of Athens, intrigued by its myriad of philosophical thoughts. He became a disciple of several philosophers, assimilating various teachings and honing his thinking. From the Stoics, he learned the importance of equanimity and self-control, from the Cynics, the significance of living in accordance with nature, and from the Platonists, he gathered knowledge about logic and metaphysics.

Zeno's philosophical journey was not linear; it was a richly textured path, laden with a synthesis of eclectic thoughts. He was not content with merely becoming a passive recipient of knowledge; instead, he actively engaged with these philosophical teachings, questioning, refining, and sometimes even challenging them. This active intellectual engagement, coupled with his resilient spirit, shaped Zeno's distinctive philosophical outlook and eventually led to the birth of Stoicism.

Zeno's philosophy, Stoicism, was born out of his realization that existing philosophies failed to offer a holistic and practical approach to life. Some philosophical schools excessively focused on metaphysics and logic but offered little advice on ethical conduct, while others, like Cynicism, promoted an ascetic life, detached from societal norms and pleasures. Zeno saw the need for a philosophy that harmonized logic, physics, and ethics and offered a pragmatic guide to life, hence Stoicism.

Stoicism, as envisioned by Zeno, was not just a theoretical construct; it was a way of life, a philosophy that guided individuals on how to lead a virtuous life amid the tumultuous waves of fortune. He propounded the doctrine of 'apatheia' or freedom from passion, where one should strive to maintain equanimity irrespective of life's vicissitudes. This idea was deeply rooted in the premise that one can't control external circumstances but can control their reactions to them.

This principle, while seemingly simple, revolutionized the understanding of human agency. It placed the locus of control within the individual, shifting the focus from external circumstances to inner attitudes. Thus, Zeno argued, the key to happiness lies not in altering our external environment but in changing our internal responses.

The foundational principles of Stoicism, as established by Zeno, were profoundly humanistic and egalitarian. He rejected the societal hierarchies and divisions based on wealth, status, or birth and argued that all humans share a universal brotherhood, grounded in their capacity for reason. He proposed that virtue, not wealth or status, is the greatest good, and it is accessible to all regardless of their societal position. This radical notion questioned the prevailing social norms, asserting that even a slave could be more virtuous and hence superior to a non-virtuous king.

Zeno's Stoicism was transformative, not just for the individual but also for society. It encouraged individuals to actively participate in civic life and fulfill their societal duties, marking a departure from philosophies like Cynicism, which advocated for complete withdrawal from societal affairs. Zeno held that one could maintain their inner tranquility even while engaged in societal roles, making Stoicism a practical guide for both personal and social life.

The influence of Zeno's Stoicism spread far and wide, transcending the boundaries of Citium and permeating the social fabric of Rome. His teachings were embraced by individuals from all walks of life, from slaves like Epictetus to emperors like Marcus Aurelius. They found in Stoicism a practical guide to life, a philosophy that resonated with their experiences and offered solace in times of adversity.

Zeno's journey into philosophy, thus, was not merely a personal transformation; it was a transformative force that shaped the ethical, societal, and political thought of the Greco-Roman world. The principles he established continue to guide millions today, making Zeno's philosophical journey and the birth of Stoicism a remarkable testament to the enduring power of philosophy.

ZENO'S PHILOSOPHY AND TEACHINGS

Zeno of Citium was more than just the founder of Stoicism; he was an intellectual pioneer who challenged existing philosophical paradigms and crafted a unique philosophical doctrine that continues to resonate with people across the millennia. His teachings, grounded in the bedrock of reason and virtue, provided a guide to living a fulfilling and tranquil life, irrespective of one's external circumstances. This section will delve into the intricacies of Zeno's philosophy and teachings, highlighting their distinct aspects and their foundational role in Stoic philosophy.

Zeno's philosophical journey was catalyzed by the eclectic intellectual environment of Athens. The teachings of the Cynics, the Stoics, and the Platonists had a profound impact on his thinking. He engaged with these philosophical doctrines, absorbing their insights, questioning their assumptions, and synthesizing them into a unique philosophical system that came to be known as Stoicism. Zeno's Stoicism was characterized by a holistic approach that harmoniously integrated logic, physics, and ethics, providing a comprehensive guide to understanding the world and navigating life.

At the heart of Zeno's philosophy was the concept of 'Logos.' Derived from the Stoics, Logos referred to the rational principle governing the universe. Zeno envisaged the universe as an orderly entity, underpinned by Logos, which manifests itself in the laws of nature and human reason. He postulated that to lead a virtuous and fulfilled life, one must align oneself with the Logos, living in accordance with nature and reason. This principle served as the cornerstone of Stoicism, guiding the Stoic view of ethics, physics, and logic.

In the realm of ethics, Zeno championed the doctrine of 'apatheia,' or freedom from passion. He posited that human suffering stems from our desires and fears, our irrational attachments to external things beyond our control. He argued that to achieve 'apatheia,' one must differentiate between what is within our control—our judgments, intentions, and reactions—and what is not—external circumstances. By focusing on what is within our control and maintaining equanimity towards what is not, we can attain tranquility and freedom from suffering.

This Stoic principle of control exerted a profound influence on ethical thinking, shifting the focus from external outcomes to internal attitudes. It established that our happiness and tranquility are not dependent on external things but on our judgments and reactions. This insight has proven to be a powerful tool for resilience and mental well-being, equipping individuals with the psychological strength to face adversities.

Moreover, Zeno's philosophy underscored the importance of virtue, positing it as the sole good and the key to a fulfilled life. Virtue, in Zeno's view, was not a static state but a dynamic process of living in accordance with nature and reason. It involved acting rightly, guided by wisdom, courage, justice, and temperance. He held that a virtuous life leads to 'eudaimonia,' a state of fulfilled and flourishing life. This Stoic view of virtue and 'eudaimonia' has had a lasting impact on ethical philosophy, influencing thinkers from the Roman Stoics to modern virtue ethicists.

On the physical front, Zeno's philosophy embraced a deterministic view of the universe, governed by the Logos. He held that everything in the universe is interconnected and determined by a chain of cause and effect. This deterministic worldview, however, did not negate human agency. Zeno asserted that while we can't change the course of events, we have the freedom to choose our responses, a freedom grounded in our rational nature.

Furthermore, Zeno's Stoicism proposed a pantheistic view of divinity. God, according to Zeno, was not a personal deity but the Logos pervading the universe. He argued that the divine and the natural are not separate entities, but one and the same, a view that challenged the anthropocentric conceptions of divinity and fostered a deep reverence for nature.

In the realm of logic, Zeno's Stoicism was marked by a rigorous approach to reasoning and argumentation. He emphasized the importance of clear thinking and sound judgment in discerning the truth and making ethical decisions. The Stoic logic, formulated by Zeno and his successors, was a formidable intellectual tool that strengthened the

Stoic ethical and physical doctrines and protected them from sophistical attacks.

Zeno's philosophy and teachings, thus, offered a profound and comprehensive guide to life, a guide that harmonized the physical, logical, and ethical dimensions of existence. His Stoicism provided a roadmap to a fulfilled life, empowering individuals with the wisdom to navigate the world with equanimity and virtue. The principles he laid out—living in accordance with nature and reason, focusing on what is within our control, and valuing virtue above all—continue to guide millions, demonstrating the enduring relevance and vitality of Zeno's philosophy.

Zeno's philosophical legacy transcends the confines of Citium or the period he lived in; it is a timeless beacon of wisdom that illuminates the path to a tranquil and virtuous life. His teachings resonate with us today, not merely as historical relics but as living principles that help us cope with the uncertainties and challenges of modern life. The exploration of Zeno's philosophy and teachings thus offers not just an insight into the origins of Stoicism, but also a guide to leading a fulfilling life in today's world.

THE LEGACY OF ZENO

Zeno of Citium, the progenitor of Stoicism, left an indelible mark on the philosophical landscape, shaping the intellectual trajectory of the Hellenistic period and beyond. His legacy permeates through the centuries, reverberating in the thoughts of numerous philosophers and common people alike, who found solace and guidance in his teachings. Even today, his ideas and principles continue to resonate, influencing modern discourse on ethics, resilience, and the art of living.

Zeno's immediate impact was on his successors, who carried forward and developed his Stoic philosophy. Stoic luminaries such as Cleanthes, Chrysippus, Seneca, Epictetus, and Marcus Aurelius, among others, drew from Zeno's teachings, further refining the Stoic doctrine. They propagated the principles he laid out, adding their insights, and thereby ensuring Stoicism's continued vitality. Zeno's teachings, thus, permeated the Hellenistic and Roman world, shaping the ethical, physical, and logical discourse of these societies.

Beyond the Stoic school, Zeno's influence extended to other philosophical schools. His ideas about logic, metaphysics, and ethics sparked debates and discussions, challenging and enriching various philosophical doctrines. Furthermore, his teachings also found echoes in early Christian thought, particularly in the concept of 'apatheia' or equanimity, and the emphasis on virtue.

In the modern world, Zeno's legacy is palpable in the burgeoning interest in Stoic philosophy. His teachings about living in accordance with nature and reason, differentiating between what is within our control and what is not, and valuing virtue above all, find relevance in a world grappling with complexity and uncertainty. These Stoic principles, rooted in Zeno's philosophy, have found applications in various fields, from cognitive-behavioral therapy to leadership training, from resilience-building to self-improvement.

Moreover, Zeno's philosophical journey, from a shipwrecked merchant to the founder of a significant philosophical school, continues to inspire individuals, embodying the transformative power of philosophy. His life story serves as a testament to the human capacity for resilience, intellectual growth, and ethical development, further amplifying his enduring legacy.

In conclusion, Zeno's legacy is not confined to his contributions to Stoic philosophy. He was a luminary whose teachings transcended his time, influencing diverse philosophical traditions and continuing to inspire and guide individuals on their path to virtue and fulfillment.

———

In assessing the pantheon of Stoicism, the life and teachings of Zeno of Citium command a special place. His unique trajectory from a merchant to the founder of one of the most influential philosophical schools in history is a compelling narrative of resilience, intellectual curiosity, and moral quest.

Zeno's philosophical precepts formed the bedrock of Stoic philosophy. They emerged as a beacon of wisdom guiding individuals to lead virtuous, fulfilled lives, irrespective of external circumstances. His teachings transcend time, remaining as relevant and insightful in our contemporary world as they were during the Hellenistic period.

In summary, the importance of Zeno to Stoicism and philosophy at large cannot be overstated. His pioneering ideas have had a profound influence on thinkers, leaders, and truth-seekers across epochs. As we venture further into the exploration of Stoic philosophy and its principal proponents, we carry forward the insights gleaned from Zeno's life and teachings, a true testament to his enduring legacy.

CHAPTER 10
CHRYSIPPUS - THE SECOND FOUNDER OF STOICISM

C hrysippus of Soli, often referred to as the "Second Founder of Stoicism," was a pivotal figure in the development and systematization of Stoic philosophy. Born in 279 BCE in Soli, Cilicia, now modern-day Turkey, Chrysippus's intellectual contributions were so significant that the Stoic school might have dissolved without his work. Even though little of his writing remains today, his reputation as a formidable philosopher is well acknowledged, having penned more than 700 works during his lifetime.

Chrysippus's formative years were not marked by philosophical pursuits. Instead, he was initially devoted to athletics, demonstrating prowess in long-distance running. However, his path changed dramatically after a chance encounter with Cleanthes, the then head of the Stoic school and a direct successor to Stoicism's founder, Zeno of Citium. Intrigued by Stoic philosophy's principles, Chrysippus chose to immerse himself in the discipline, thereby forever changing his life and, ultimately, the trajectory of Stoic philosophy.

What distinguishes Chrysippus is not merely his dedication to Stoic philosophy but his efforts to refine, expand, and defend it. He was instrumental in developing a comprehensive system of Stoic logic, a crucial aspect of the philosophy that came to be highly regarded in antiquity. Furthermore, he made significant contributions to Stoic ethics and physics, formulating doctrines that would be integral to Stoicism.

To comprehend the magnitude of Chrysippus's contributions, one must grasp the state of Stoicism before his intervention. While Zeno of Citium laid Stoicism's foundation, the philosophy still lacked systematization. Chrysippus recognized this need and set out to fortify Stoicism by organizing its concepts into a cohesive whole. Through his arduous intellectual work, Chrysippus helped Stoicism survive and thrive in a competitive philosophical landscape.

His enduring legacy is reflected in the oft-repeated saying, "But for Chrysippus, there had been no Porch," the Porch referring to the Stoa Poikile, the Athenian colonnade where Stoics gathered and the school derived its name. This aphorism encapsulates Chrysippus's importance as the savior of Stoicism, a philosopher whose rigorous intellectual work cemented Stoicism's place in philosophical discourse. Even centuries after his passing, the echoes of Chrysippus's influence continue to resound in Stoic philosophy and its modern interpretations.

EARLY LIFE AND PATH TO STOICISM

Chrysippus's early life and philosophical journey embody a transformational narrative of shifting from athletics to the intellectual rigor of Stoic philosophy. His birthplace, Soli, was a thriving center of Hellenistic culture in Cilicia, located in the southern part of modern-day Turkey. Born into a wealthy family in 279 BCE, Chrysippus had the means and leisure to engage in a variety of pursuits. In his youth, he showed a keen interest in athletics, particularly excelling in long-distance running. This early inclination towards physical endurance perhaps hints at his later mental perseverance in intellectual fields.

In terms of his education, little is known, but it can be assumed that being a member of an affluent family, he would have received a well-rounded education characteristic of Hellenistic culture. He likely studied a wide range of subjects, including literature, music, and a variety of physical disciplines.

Despite the initial focus on physical pursuits, Chrysippus's life took a significant turn when he chanced upon the teachings of Stoic philosophy. Some sources suggest that he was introduced to philosophy by Cleanthes, the then head of the Stoic school. Under Cleanthes, the Stoic school was struggling to sustain itself due to Cleanthes's limited intellectual capabilities. Intrigued by the ideas of Stoicism and perhaps sensing the need for a capable mind to support the school, Chrysippus decided to immerse himself in the study of philosophy.

Chrysippus's decision to abandon athletics for philosophy is illustrative of his adaptive spirit and the courage to pursue his intellectual interests. It also demonstrates a distinctive feature of Stoicism: the idea that the pursuit of wisdom is the highest form of human endeavor, surpassing physical achievements.

Upon entering the Stoic school, Chrysippus embarked on a rigorous program of study. He showed immense dedication and intellectual curiosity, quickly becoming Cleanthes's most promising student. His commitment to Stoicism and his astonishing intellectual capacity made him the natural successor to Cleanthes as the head of the Stoic school.

Chrysippus's move to Stoicism represented a significant shift in his personal worldview. Stoicism, with its emphasis on virtue, tranquility, and the acceptance of fate, provided a philosophical framework that resonated deeply with him. It offered him a way to navigate life's ups and downs with equanimity. The teachings of Stoicism, which emphasized the need for individuals to live in accordance with nature and reason, allowed Chrysippus to lead a life of intellectual pursuit and moral virtue.

His path to Stoicism is a testament to the philosophy's broad appeal to individuals from diverse backgrounds and interests. Even today, many are drawn to Stoicism because of its practical approach to life's challenges, and Chrysippus stands as an example of the transformative power of Stoic philosophy. His transition from an athlete to a philosopher highlights Stoicism's inherent flexibility and its potential to guide individuals towards a life of wisdom and tranquility.

As he delved deeper into Stoic teachings, Chrysippus began to recognize the need for further development and systematization of the philosophy. While the foundational ideas of Stoicism were laid out by Zeno, the philosophy was still in its infancy and faced the risk of dissolution. Recognizing this, Chrysippus embarked on an ambitious project to develop Stoicism into a more robust and comprehensive philosophy.

His transition from an athlete to the Second Founder of Stoicism is not just a tale of personal transformation but also a story of the growth of Stoicism itself. It reflects how Stoicism, as a philosophy, was adaptable and capable of evolving and growing over time.

Chrysippus's early life and journey to Stoicism underscore the transformative power of philosophy. His story is an enduring reminder of the power of the human mind to engage with complex ideas and contribute to their development, thereby influencing generations of thinkers and shaping the course of philosophical history.

CHRYSIPPUS'S PHILOSOPHICAL JOURNEY

As Chrysippus delved into the philosophical realm, he embarked on a journey that led him to re-examine and significantly contribute to Stoic doctrine. His intellect and unparalleled productivity – with over 705 works to his name – solidified his influence on Stoicism. Despite the loss of his original writings, fragments preserved in later works testify to his philosophical genius.

The body of Stoic philosophy consists of three intertwined parts: logic, physics, and ethics, often depicted as a fertile field (ethics), surrounded by a protective wall (physics), and buttressed by the rampart of a castle (logic). Zeno laid the foundation, but Chrysippus honed and systematized these aspects, making them more defensible and coherent.

Stoic logic, which covers the theory of knowledge and formal logic, received significant contributions from Chrysippus. Rejecting the Platonic-Aristotelian idea of abstract entities, he proposed a novel theory of cognition centered on mental impressions. For Chrysippus, knowledge was certainty, an unchangeable conviction founded on the cognitive impression, which is an imprint of reality on the soul. Thus, it harmonizes epistemology with the Stoic materialist metaphysics. His advancements in propositional logic, particularly the logical connectives and the system of 'if-then' (implicational) logic, were groundbreaking, rivaling Aristotle's syllogistic.

In the realm of physics, which the Stoics understood as a rational explanation of the universe, Chrysippus further elaborated the pantheistic worldview. He viewed the cosmos as a rational, animate, and divine entity. God was the fiery reason (logos) inherent in the universe, causing its eternal cycle of destruction and regeneration. While Zeno had initially posited the theory of cosmic determinism, Chrysippus elucidated it, maintaining that everything occurs according to an interconnected chain of causes and effects. This philosophy of causal determinism fortified the Stoic exhortation to accept one's fate calmly.

Furthermore, Chrysippus's philosophical explorations led him to refine Stoic ethics, which was about living in accordance with nature. He insisted that the only good was virtue, the perfect rationality, and everything else was indifferent. However, he introduced the concept of 'preferred' and 'dispreferred', bridging the seemingly insurmountable gap between the lofty Stoic wisdom and daily life. For instance, while wealth or health was not good in itself, it was preferable to its opposite if it did not compromise virtue.

His treatment of emotions as misguided judgments rather than uncontrollable forces was particularly innovative. He theorized that humans could eradicate destructive passions by replacing false beliefs about what's good or bad with the right Stoic knowledge. This emotional therapy offered practical guidance for individuals to attain tranquility (ataraxia), the ultimate goal of Stoic ethics.

Undoubtedly, Chrysippus was a pivotal figure in the Stoic school. His extensive contributions to Stoic philosophy helped shape it into a comprehensive system of thought that could rival other Hellenistic schools like Epicureanism and Skepticism. Despite the obscurity that shrouds his original works, the fragments that remain still demonstrate a rigorous philosophical system that has influenced thinkers throughout the centuries.

Chrysippus's philosophical journey is emblematic of a mind wholly dedicated to the pursuit of wisdom. It is a journey that took Stoicism from a burgeoning philosophical movement to a fully formed school of thought that has endured for over two millennia. His contributions to Stoic philosophy not only deepened its richness but also enhanced its appeal, making it a compelling philosophical system that continues to captivate minds today.

CHRYSIPPUS'S PHILOSOPHY AND TEACHINGS

Chrysippus's philosophical teachings encompassed a vast spectrum of concepts, themes, and theories, forming the bedrock of Stoicism. As a prolific writer and philosopher, he extended and refined the Stoic thought initially established by Zeno, cementing Stoicism as a signifi-cant philosophical school in the Hellenistic era. To understand the depth of his intellectual rigor and the breadth of his influence, it is essential to delve into his key philosophical teachings and analyze their relevance in both historical and contemporary contexts.

Chrysippus's contributions to logic, a major component of Stoicism, were pivotal. He is most renowned for his development of proposi-tional or 'sentential' logic, which revolved around the logical relations of propositions or statements. His system of logic was highly advanced for its time and is often regarded as an early precursor to modern symbolic and mathematical logic. Many of Chrysippus's logical inno-vations, including his use of truth tables and his work on conditionals and conjunctions, laid the groundwork for later logicians.

His teaching that knowledge was certainty, an unchangeable conviction founded on the cognitive impression, was a major develop-ment. Cognitive impressions, according to Chrysippus, are infallible and formed the basis of knowledge. This perspective laid the founda-tion for the Stoic concept of knowledge, which emphasized a clear and distinct perception of the external world. This theory remains relevant, particularly in modern discussions on the theory of knowledge and the nature of perception. Chrysippus's teachings on logic also have contemporary relevance in the fields of computer science and artificial intelligence, both of which rely heavily on logical systems.

Chrysippus's teachings also significantly expanded Stoic physics, which broadly encompassed natural philosophy. His pantheistic worldview, which equated God with the cosmos's rational principle or logos, was a fundamental part of this. Chrysippus saw the universe as a rational, living entity with God as its animating principle. This view not only offered an explanation for the world's natural phenomena but also provided comfort and purpose to individuals facing life's hardships.

Furthermore, Chrysippus extensively developed the Stoic doctrine of determinism. His belief that everything happens according to Fate or an interconnected chain of cause and effect was revolutionary. He likened the universe to a well-trained dog tied to a cart; the dog could either follow the cart willingly or be dragged along. Similarly, humans could either accept their fate willingly, thereby achieving peace of mind, or resist it and suffer. These teachings are highly relevant today, as the discussion around free will and determinism continues in philosophical and scientific circles.

Ethics, the central and most practical component of Stoic philosophy, was another domain where Chrysippus's teachings were substantial. His views on virtue, the supreme good, and human happiness provide practical guidance that still resonates today. For Chrysippus, virtue was the only good, the perfect rationality, and living in accordance with virtue was the path to happiness. But, understanding the complexities of human life, he introduced the concept of 'preferred' and 'dispreferred' indifferents, thus making Stoic philosophy more accessible and applicable.

One of his most significant ethical teachings was the concept of emotions as misguided judgments, asserting that destructive passions resulted from false beliefs about what is good and bad. This teaching has resonated through the centuries, finding echoes in cognitive-behavioral therapy (CBT), a modern psychological treatment approach that involves changing thought patterns to alter feelings and behavior.

Chrysippus's teachings serve as a testimony to his intellectual prowess and his deep understanding of human nature and the natural world. His philosophy, despite being articulated over two millennia ago, still holds profound relevance in the modern world. His contributions to logic, physics, and ethics continue to influence philosophical discourse, offer therapeutic wisdom, and provide a lens through which to view and navigate the complexities of life.

Whether we're wrestling with issues of determinism and free will, trying to understand the relationship between the universe and the divine, or seeking practical guidance for leading virtuous and fulfilling lives, Chrysippus's philosophy offers profound insights. It serves as a reminder that despite the immense advances in science and technology, the fundamental questions of life, reality, and morality remain much the same as they were in Chrysippus's time.

In conclusion, the teachings of Chrysippus form a significant part of the rich tapestry of Stoic philosophy. They provide us with a robust framework for understanding the world around us, navigating life's challenges, and striving towards virtue and wisdom. Whether we examine his philosophy from a historical, intellectual, or practical standpoint, the importance and relevance of Chrysippus's teachings are undeniable.

THE LEGACY OF CHRYSIPPUS

Chrysippus, often hailed as the Second Founder of Stoicism, left a legacy that continues to shape the understanding and practice of Stoic philosophy today. Although much of his original writings are lost, his philosophical teachings, available through secondary sources, have echoed through the centuries, forming a bridge between the early Stoic thought initiated by Zeno and the later Stoicism of the Roman era.

The influence of Chrysippus is particularly evident in the field of logic. His intricate and advanced system of propositional logic, with its focus on the logical relations of statements, underpinned the Stoic school's intellectual rigor. It laid a foundation for logical thinking that resonates even today in modern logic, computer science, and artificial intelligence. This monumental contribution earned him a lasting place in the annals of philosophy and the broader scientific world.

In Stoic physics and cosmology, Chrysippus's pantheistic worldview that equated the divine with the rational principle of the cosmos presented a distinctive interpretation of reality. His profound belief in determinism, the interconnected chain of cause and effect, has provided much food for thought in the ongoing debate around free will, determinism, and the nature of the universe.

But perhaps Chrysippus's most enduring legacy is his practical philosophy, which still finds relevance today. His teachings on emotions as misguided judgments have deeply influenced modern psychotherapy, particularly Cognitive Behavioral Therapy, which emphasizes the role of thoughts in influencing feelings and behavior.

Moreover, his conceptualization of virtue as the only good and the primary source of human happiness remains a cornerstone of Stoic thought and continues to inspire individuals seeking guidance and tranquillity in the tumult of life. By introducing the concept of preferred and dispreferred indifferents, he humanized Stoicism, making it more accessible and practical.

Overall, Chrysippus's legacy is profound and enduring. His philosophical teachings have not only shaped Stoicism but continue to influence modern thought across various disciplines. His philosophical perspective offers timeless wisdom and practical insights that guide many in their quest for a balanced and meaningful life.

———

Chrysippus's remarkable life and teachings occupy a pivotal place in the narrative of Stoicism. As we reflect upon his vast contributions, it is apparent that he not only deepened and solidified the teachings of his predecessors, but also innovated and expanded Stoic philosophy in ways that continue to reverberate.

His groundbreaking work in logic, physics, ethics, and cosmology set a high bar for intellectual rigor and moral guidance. His unique blend of rationalism, humanism, and deep reverence for nature's inherent wisdom offers a vision of Stoicism that is comprehensive, grounded, and profoundly resonant with our human condition. It is through his philosophical lens that we gain a holistic understanding of Stoicism as not merely a philosophical school, but as a way of life.

As we transition to the next chapter, we will delve into the lives and philosophies of other Stoics who continued the tradition that Chrysippus so ardently advanced. The insights they offer will further our exploration of Stoicism, deepening our understanding of its timeless wisdom and contemporary relevance.

CHAPTER 11
CLEANTHES - THE
TORCHBEARER OF STOICISM

Cleanthes of Assos, often lesser-known yet a formidable figure in the history of Stoic philosophy, is most renowned for succeeding Zeno of Citium as the scholarch, or head, of the Stoic school. Born in 330 BC, in the seaport town of Assos in the Troad region of Asia Minor, he was a contemporary of many great Hellenistic thinkers and witnessed firsthand the era that profoundly shaped Western philosophical thought.

From an early age, Cleanthes was not a stranger to hard work and perseverance. His upbringing in Assos was humble, with his father being a boxer. This simple life would soon lead Cleanthes to Athens, where he was initially tasked with the humble and strenuous job of watering the gardens at night. However, it was his extraordinary determination and curiosity that led him to the teachings of Zeno, the founder of Stoicism. Despite his limited resources, Cleanthes endeavored to pay for his lessons by continuing his water-carrying job, earning him the nickname "Phreantles," meaning "well drawer."

Cleanthes' passion for knowledge and his relentless pursuit of wisdom set him apart, bringing him to the attention of Zeno himself. The Stoic school, at the time, was a burgeoning hub of philosophical discourse, marked by rigorous intellectual debate and the collective pursuit of wisdom. Under Zeno's guidance, Cleanthes absorbed and imbibed the tenets of Stoicism, which, over time, he would come to shape in his distinctive way.

As the successor to Zeno, Cleanthes held the mantle of leadership for an impressive 32 years, from 263 BC until his death in 232 BC. Although he lived in the shadow of his formidable predecessor, Cleanthes proved himself a dedicated custodian of the Stoic tradition. He did not merely replicate Zeno's teachings but brought his own interpretations and contributions to the fore. Cleanthes' Stoicism was characterized by an unwavering belief in divine providence, a theme he beautifully expressed in his famous "Hymn to Zeus."

While not a prolific writer – only fragments of his works have survived – Cleanthes was known for his integrity, simplicity, and his strict adherence to the Stoic way of life. His contemporaries often noted his lifestyle, which starkly contrasted the often-privileged lives of other philosophers of his time. To Cleanthes, philosophy was not merely a subject of intellectual discourse but a way of life, a guide to ethical living, to be embodied in thought, word, and deed.

It would be misleading, however, to define Cleanthes merely by his ascetic lifestyle or his hard work. His importance in Stoicism cannot be overstated. As the scholarch following Zeno, Cleanthes played a crucial role in preserving and propelling Stoic philosophy during its early, formative years. He was instrumental in steering the Stoic school during a critical phase and shaped it into a potent philosophical force that would go on to have a profound impact on the Western intellectual tradition. It was his commitment to Stoicism, his dedicated leadership, and his unique philosophical contributions that carved his indelible place in the annals of Stoic philosophy.

The life of Cleanthes embodies the Stoic virtues of courage, justice, wisdom, and moderation. Despite the odds, he rose from a humble gardener to lead one of the most influential schools of philosophy in history. Through his life and work, Cleanthes exemplifies the spirit of Stoicism and stands as a testament to the philosophy's enduring principles. As we delve deeper into his life, his teachings, and his enduring legacy, we continue to unravel the significant role Cleanthes played in shaping Stoic philosophy.

With the passing of time, the torch of Stoicism passed on from Zeno to Cleanthes, and eventually to others. Each torchbearer added their distinctive strokes to the Stoic canvas. As we explore Cleanthes' unique contributions to Stoic philosophy, we find his life and teachings a valuable lesson in understanding and practicing Stoicism, both then and now.

EARLY LIFE AND PATH TO STOICISM

The early life of Cleanthes provides a rich narrative, laden with trials, perseverance, and ultimately, philosophical enlightenment. Born in 330 BC, in the ancient city of Assos, Cleanthes grew up amid the bustling seaport town's simplicity and stark realities. The environment provided a strong work ethic, instilling in him early on a profound sense of discipline and humility. Unlike many philosophers of his time, Clenches did not come from a background of privilege or scholarly lineage. His father was a boxer, and the family was of modest means.

The toughness of his early life served as a crucible, shaping and refining his character. The arduous physical labor he was accustomed to in his youth didn't cease when he moved to Athens. His initial employment in the city was as a water-carrier, a task he undertook during the nocturnal hours. Even as he engaged in his laborious work, Cleanthes nurtured a burning desire for knowledge. This yearning led him to the doorstep of the Stoic school where Zeno was imparting his philosophical teachings.

According to the historian Diogenes Laërtius, Cleanthes arrived at Athens with only four drachmas to his name. Nevertheless, he was determined to study under Zeno, even if it meant continuing his backbreaking labor to fund his education. This determination and willingness to persevere under challenging circumstances caught Zeno's attention, who began to see Cleanthes as a potential successor.

His early exposure to the rigors of life significantly influenced Cleanthes's perspective, enabling him to embrace Stoicism's core tenets wholeheartedly. Stoicism's emphasis on virtues like wisdom, courage, justice, and temperance resonated deeply with him. The philosophy's call for living in accordance with nature and accepting life's vicissitudes with grace and resilience echoed his personal experiences.

Cleanthes's journey towards Stoicism was not a result of chance but a choice born out of deep conviction. Stoicism's core teaching, that virtue is the only true good and that our will is completely in our control, found a willing disciple in Cleanthes. His early life's trials and tribulations did not embitter him but made him a steadfast proponent of Stoic philosophy.

His journey from Assos to Athens, from a water-carrier to the head of the Stoic school, is a narrative marked by resolute perseverance, humility, and a relentless pursuit of wisdom. Cleanthes, the laborer-turned-philosopher, stands as an embodiment of Stoic virtues, demonstrating that the pursuit of wisdom is not confined to the academically privileged or the socially elite.

Cleanthes' early life and his path to Stoicism are testament to his indomitable spirit and unwavering commitment to philosophy. His personal life was a reflection of his philosophical convictions - a life lived in simplicity, resilience, and virtue. His teachings were not mere intellectual exercises but lessons drawn from his life, steeped in the harsh realities and experiences he had lived through.

His philosophical journey, from an eager student to a revered teacher, exemplifies the transformative power of Stoicism. It offers a deep and profound understanding of Stoic philosophy's practicality, emphasizing its relevance beyond the academic realm and demonstrating its applicability in daily life.

In Cleanthes, we see the fusion of the philosophical and the practical, the merging of thought and action, the embodiment of Stoicism's core tenets. His life, characterized by its stark simplicity and dogged determination, offers invaluable insights into the philosophy he upheld and propagated. As we delve further into the life and teachings of Cleanthes, we continue to uncover the timeless relevance and profound wisdom of Stoic philosophy.

CLEANTHES'S PHILOSOPHICAL JOURNEY

Cleanthes' ascension as the head of the Stoic school following Zeno's death marked a significant phase in his philosophical journey. Despite initial criticism due to his lack of formal education, Cleanthes quickly silenced detractors with his insightful contributions to Stoic philosophy and proved to be a worthy successor. As head of the Stoic school, Cleanthes faced the daunting task of building upon Zeno's foundational work and steering the course of Stoicism during its formative years.

Cleanthes distinguished himself by expanding and consolidating Zeno's teachings. His lack of traditional education actually worked in his favor as he brought a fresh perspective to Stoic philosophy. He was not bound by the traditional methodologies of philosophy, enabling him to approach Stoic doctrine in innovative ways.

One of Cleanthes' significant contributions was in the realm of Stoic physics, where he proposed his "two principles" doctrine. He contended that the universe operates through the interaction of two principles: one passive, which he equated to matter, and one active, equated to reason or divine intellect. The interplay of these principles resulted in the creation and operation of the universe.

He also furthered the Stoic understanding of Logos, a concept introduced by Heraclitus and adopted by Stoics as a term to describe the rational principle governing the universe. Cleanthes offered a more spiritual interpretation of Logos, associating it with divine reason or God. He saw Logos as a divine fire or breath that infused the universe, shaping and directing all things according to rational laws.

On the ethical front, Cleanthes is famously associated with the Stoic doctrine of "following nature." While this was a cornerstone of Stoic philosophy, Cleanthes added a new dimension to it. He emphasized that "following nature" meant not just accepting the external events determined by fate but also aspiring to the rational principle that governed the cosmos. For Cleanthes, the virtuous life was one where human will was aligned with the divine will or Logos.

Cleanthes' philosophical journey was also marked by his contributions to Stoic theology. His famous "Hymn to Zeus" is a testament to his religious devotion and his belief in a rational, providential deity guiding the universe. The hymn not only offers a glimpse into his personal spirituality but also encapsulates key Stoic concepts such as the divine Logos, providence, and the importance of living in accordance with nature.

In addition to his substantial contributions to Stoic doctrine, Cleanthes' tenure as head of the Stoic school is noteworthy for his teaching style. He encouraged his students to engage critically with Stoic teachings rather than merely accepting them. His pedagogical approach reflected the Stoic belief in the importance of reason and independent thought, further reinforcing the philosophy's intellectual rigor.

Despite his early struggles, Cleanthes' philosophical journey is a testament to his tenacity, intellectual curiosity, and steadfast commitment to Stoicism. His interpretations and expansions of Zeno's teachings, while sometimes criticized, were instrumental in shaping the course of Stoicism. Through his work, Cleanthes helped ensure that Stoicism was not merely a philosophy of abstract ideas but a practical guide to virtuous living.

Cleanthes' life and philosophical journey demonstrate that wisdom and insight can arise from the most challenging circumstances. His contributions to Stoic philosophy, both as a thinker and as a teacher, serve as a lasting testament to his intellectual legacy. He not only carried the torch of Stoicism following Zeno's death but also added his own distinctive light to its illuminating path.

CLEANTHES'S PHILOSOPHY AND TEACHINGS

To truly appreciate Cleanthes's philosophical teachings, it is necessary to delve into his contributions across the fields of physics, ethics, and theology within Stoic philosophy. Cleanthes played a vital role in developing and refining these philosophical strands, lending his unique insights to each domain and shaping Stoic thought in significant ways.

The sphere of Stoic physics benefited greatly from Cleanthes' doctrine of the "two principles". In essence, this doctrine suggested that the universe operates through the active and passive interplay of two principles. The passive principle corresponded to matter, which was receptive to the formative influence of the active principle—reason or divine intellect. This model posited a universe infused with rationality at its most fundamental level, a universe where every occurrence could be understood as the outcome of rational principles at work.

Furthermore, Cleanthes contributed a noteworthy interpretation of the Stoic concept of Logos. Originally introduced by Heraclitus, Logos was adopted by Stoics as a term for the rational principle governing the universe. Cleanthes deepened this concept with a more spiritual nuance, associating Logos with divine reason or God. He saw Logos as a divine fire or breath infusing and directing the universe in accordance with rational laws. This idea effectively merged the physical and the divine, positioning the universe as a manifestation of divine reason and order.

His thoughts on Logos significantly influenced Stoic theology, evident in his well-known "Hymn to Zeus." This hymn reflects Cleanthes' devout belief in a rational, providential deity that guides the universe. Simultaneously, it encapsulates key Stoic ideas—the divine Logos, providence, and living in accordance with nature—making it a remarkable poetic synthesis of Stoic thought.

In the realm of Stoic ethics, Cleanthes is most closely associated with the doctrine of "following nature". Although this was a central Stoic idea, Cleanthes added a profound dimension to it. For him, "following nature" was not just passive acceptance of external events but also an aspiration to align one's will with the divine will or Logos. Cleanthes' view presents virtue as living in harmony with the rational order of the universe, a perspective that gives Stoic ethics its distinctively cosmopolitan character.

Historically, Cleanthes's philosophy and teachings, particularly his belief in divine providence and the importance of living according to nature, had considerable influence. His ideas permeated the Stoic school, impacting subsequent generations of Stoics, and his thoughts on divine providence resonated with Christian thinkers, contributing to the development of Christian theology.

In a modern context, Cleanthes's teachings hold relevance in several ways. His belief in a rational, ordered universe resonates with our scientific understanding of the cosmos, where natural laws govern all phenomena. His views on ethics, especially the doctrine of "following nature", find resonance in contemporary discussions about environmental ethics and sustainable living. Moreover, his emphasis on aligning one's will with the larger rational order speaks to the modern pursuit of purpose and the desire for harmony with the larger world.

To interpret and explain Cleanthes' philosophical legacy, it is important to acknowledge his unique role within Stoic philosophy. He wasn't just a passive torchbearer, merely perpetuating Zeno's teachings; he was an active thinker, contributing crucial ideas and interpretations to Stoicism. His contributions underscore the dynamic nature of Stoic philosophy, reminding us that Stoicism was not a static doctrine but a living, evolving philosophical tradition.

Cleanthes was not without his critics, both among his contemporaries and in subsequent generations. Some questioned his unconventional approach to philosophical inquiry, while others criticized his spiritual interpretation of Logos. Yet, despite these criticisms, Cleanthes's teachings hold a valuable place in the Stoic canon. His thoughts on the physical universe, divine providence, and ethical living represent some of the central pillars of Stoic philosophy, shaping the tradition in significant ways and continuing to offer insightful perspectives for modern readers.

THE LEGACY OF CLEANTHES

Cleanthes, often recognized as the diligent torchbearer of Stoicism, etched his place in the philosophical world through his novel interpretations and deepened understanding of Stoic doctrine. His influence extends far beyond his tenure as the head of the Stoic school; his teachings continue to shape Stoicism, contributing to its evolution and relevance.

Cleanthes's view of the Logos as a divine force, a principle that infuses and directs the universe, added a spiritual dimension to Stoicism, which had lasting implications. This belief in a providential, rational deity, which he eloquently expressed in his "Hymn to Zeus," infused Stoicism with a sense of the sacred. This perspective arguably contributed to Stoicism's appeal in the Roman world and helped bridge the gap between Stoic philosophy and the emerging Christian doctrine.

Moreover, Cleanthes's unique spin on the doctrine of "following nature" provided a fresh lens through which to understand and practice Stoic ethics. By conceptualizing the idea of living according to nature as aligning one's will with the divine Logos, Cleanthes lent an aspirational quality to Stoic ethics that resonated deeply within the tradition and beyond.

In addition, Cleanthes's contributions to Stoic physics—the doctrine of the two principles and his view of the universe as a manifestation of divine reason—provided a firm groundwork for subsequent Stoic thinkers. His ideas still resonate today, particularly in discussions on the harmony between science and spirituality.

Cleanthes's legacy lives on in the philosophy he helped shape. Even today, his teachings continue to offer insights, resonating with those seeking to navigate life with resilience, tranquility, and a sense of purpose. His interpretations of Stoic doctrine emphasize harmony— with the self, the community, and the cosmos—making his legacy a profoundly enriching facet of Stoicism.

While his writings may not have survived the test of time, his ideas, his profound interpretations, and his unwavering commitment to the Stoic philosophy ensure that Cleanthes's spirit continues to pervade the annals of Stoic thought. By teaching us the importance of diligent learning, the pursuit of virtue, and the quest for harmony with the universe, Cleanthes's legacy remains an illuminating beacon within Stoic philosophy, casting a light that guides our understanding and practice of Stoicism to this day.

———

Cleanthes of Assos, the torchbearer of Stoicism, held the flame of this philosophical school with unwavering dedication. His commitment to Stoicism, embodied in his diligent study and humble lifestyle, made him an exemplary Stoic figure. His life serves as a reminder that

Stoicism is not merely an intellectual endeavor; it is, above all, a way of life.

As a philosopher, Cleanthes refined and expanded the teachings of his predecessor, Zeno. His unique interpretations of Stoic doctrine, particularly his emphasis on the divine Logos and his take on Stoic physics and ethics, enriched the Stoic tradition. These contributions laid the foundation for later Stoic thinkers and continue to inform modern interpretations of Stoicism.

Cleanthes's legacy is a testament to the transformative power of Stoic philosophy. His teachings, although centuries old, remain relevant, offering valuable insights for those seeking to navigate life's challenges with equanimity and virtue. Cleanthes's life and philosophy illustrate that Stoicism is not about detachment or indifference, but about living in harmony with nature, oneself, and the divine.

As we move to the next chapter, we carry with us the lessons gleaned from Cleanthes's journey. His enduring wisdom illuminates the path forward, enriching our understanding of Stoicism as we delve deeper into this vibrant philosophical tradition.

CHAPTER 12
CATO THE YOUNGER - THE STOIC OF ACTION

Marcus Porcius Cato Uticensis, known to history as Cato the Younger, stands as one of the most influential figures of the late Roman Republic. Born into a family of note, Cato distinguished himself through a life of unwavering integrity, profound courage, and steadfast commitment to Stoic principles. His tale is not only about his own persona but also a reflection of the turbulent times he lived in and how his actions resonated deeply within the social, political, and philosophical landscapes of the era.

Cato's life was a testament to the potential for Stoicism to be applied in everyday life and particularly in the realm of public service. Even amidst the tumultuous and often morally challenging arena of Roman politics, Cato stood as a paragon of virtue, adhering strictly to Stoic principles. This led him to become both a celebrated and controversial figure of his time. His inflexible approach to life and politics made him a beacon of moral clarity but also led to inevitable conflicts, marking him out as a defiant outlier in the increasingly unstable landscape of the late Roman Republic.

The philosopher Seneca once said, "Life is like a play; it's not the length but the excellence of the acting that matters." Cato the Younger was an embodiment of this sentiment, living his life like a grand play, filled with honor, virtue, and defiance. His indomitable spirit and unwavering commitment to Stoic values stand as an inspiring example for all who seek to understand and implement Stoic philosophy.

As we journey into his life and teachings, it is essential to remember that Cato was not just a philosopher in thought but, more importantly, in action. His life serves as a practical guide, a living testament to the power of Stoic virtues when put into practice in one's daily life, irrespective of the challenges that one might face.

EARLY LIFE AND PATH TO STOICISM

Born in 95 B.C.E., Cato the Younger came from a renowned family with deep roots in Roman history. His great-grandfather was Cato the Elder, a famous Stoic philosopher, military leader, and statesman known for his wisdom and moral integrity. Cato the Younger's father, Marcus Porcius Cato Licinianus, was a successful lawyer and an influential figure in his own right. Yet, Cato lost his father at a young age, leaving a void that was filled by the teachings and values instilled in him by his mother, Livia Drusa, and his philosophical tutor, Sarpedon.

Cato's formative years were marked by a strict upbringing, rooted in discipline and frugality, which would later serve as a cornerstone for his Stoic beliefs. The early death of his father made a deep impression on him, highlighting the impermanence and uncertainties of life. This realization, combined with the influence of Stoic philosophy from his tutor Sarpedon, shaped Cato's worldview and his approach to life.

His education was far from ordinary. Cato was exposed to a wide range of disciplines, from literature and history to law and philosophy, which broadened his intellectual horizons. However, it was philosophy, specifically Stoicism, that had a profound impact on his young mind. Cato found solace and guidance in Stoic philosophy, which emphasized virtue, self-control, and the acceptance of fate. These principles would become the pillars upon which Cato built his life, and they guided his actions throughout his personal and political journey.

It is important to understand that Cato did not passively absorb the Stoic teachings; he embraced them with an intense fervor and implemented them in every aspect of his life. From his modest lifestyle to his unwavering commitment to truth and justice, Cato was a living embodiment of Stoic principles. He saw himself as a guardian of Roman moral and social values, striving to live a life of virtue in an increasingly corrupt society. This made him a beacon of integrity and moral rectitude, inspiring both admiration and resentment among his contemporaries.

As he grew older, Cato's commitment to Stoicism only deepened. His belief in the Stoic concept of 'fate' and the natural order of the universe became the foundation of his political and personal philosophy. He believed that by accepting the realities of life and death and by living in accordance with nature, one could achieve true happiness and inner peace. He adopted the Stoic virtues of wisdom, courage, justice, and temperance as guiding principles in his life, never straying from them, even in the face of great adversity.

Cato was unique in his application of Stoicism, not only utilizing it as a guide for personal conduct but also incorporating it into his political ethos. For him, Stoicism was not just a philosophy; it was a way of life, a compass that pointed him towards virtue and integrity in every aspect of his life. In the volatile environment of Roman politics, Cato's unyielding adherence to Stoic principles set him apart.

As Cato stepped into adulthood, his engagement with Stoic philosophy deepened. He was known for his rigorous self-discipline and austerity, which mirrored the Stoic ideal of living in accordance with nature and rejecting material excess. Despite being part of the Roman elite, Cato led a simple life, often wearing plain clothing and abstaining from lavish feasts. These were not mere affectations; they were conscious choices rooted in his Stoic beliefs, demonstrating his commitment to living according to virtue rather than pleasure or public opinion.

Cato's journey towards Stoicism was also shaped by the socio-political milieu of his time. Rome, during his lifetime, was a republic in transition, plagued by political upheavals and moral decline. Cato saw Stoicism as a remedy to this chaos, a philosophy that could provide moral and ethical guidance. By embodying the Stoic virtues in his life and political career, Cato sought to inspire his fellow citizens and steer Rome towards stability and moral rectitude.

In his pursuit of virtue and his commitment to Stoicism, Cato became a symbol of moral integrity and steadfastness in the Roman world. His life served as a testament to the transformative power of Stoicism, showing that it was possible to live a life of virtue amidst political upheaval and moral decay. Cato's adherence to Stoic principles was not without challenges, yet he remained steadfast, demonstrating the strength and resilience of his philosophical convictions.

CATO'S PHILOSOPHICAL JOURNEY

Cato the Younger's philosophical journey is a testament to his determination to live a life guided by Stoic principles. His unwavering commitment to virtue and morality, in both his private and public lives, set him apart from many of his contemporaries in the volatile world of Roman politics. Cato was not merely a student of Stoicism; he was a living embodiment of its teachings.

Born into a family renowned for its dedication to the traditional Roman virtues of duty, loyalty, and honor, Cato's exposure to Stoicism came at a crucial time in his life. As he entered his formative years, Rome was in the throes of immense political upheaval. The stability and moral guidance he found in Stoic philosophy provided him with a compass to navigate this tumultuous period. Stoicism, with its emphasis on virtue, personal responsibility, and accepting things beyond one's control, resonated deeply with Cato. He committed himself to living out these principles, not just in theory, but in practice.

As a public figure, Cato used his influence to uphold the values he held dear. He was known for his steadfastness and incorruptibility, often standing alone against corruption and moral decay. His contemporaries recognized his commitment to Stoic principles, with Plutarch noting that he "adhered to his purpose with a resolution that nothing could shake." Cato's stoic courage was legendary, as was his discipline. He was averse to excess in all forms and committed to leading a simple, austere life, despite the wealth and luxuries available to him.

In his political career, Cato saw himself as a guardian of Roman virtue and tradition, striving to uphold these values in a time of political and moral decline. He consistently placed the welfare of the republic above personal gain, embodying the Stoic ideal of duty and service. His political decisions were not guided by ambition or desire for popularity, but by a deep sense of responsibility and commitment to the common good.

Despite the hostility and opposition he often faced, Cato remained undeterred. His resilience in the face of adversity demonstrated the Stoic principle of accepting things as they are and not as one wishes them to be. He recognized that while he could not control others' actions, he could control his responses. He chose to respond with integrity, courage, and unwavering adherence to his principles.

In his personal life, Cato was equally committed to living out his Stoic beliefs. He was known for his austere lifestyle, which was in stark contrast to the extravagance prevalent among Rome's elite. His life was a practical demonstration of the Stoic principle of living in accordance with nature, prioritizing virtue over material wealth and luxury.

Cato's adherence to Stoic principles was not without its challenges. He faced criticism and opposition, both in his public and private lives. However, he remained steadfast in his convictions, demonstrating the resilience of his philosophical beliefs. His life serves as a powerful testament to the transformative potential of Stoicism when embraced wholly and authentically.

Cato's journey illustrates the profound impact Stoic philosophy can have on an individual's life and society as a whole. His life stands as a beacon of moral integrity and virtue, illuminating the path for those seeking guidance in their own philosophical journeys. Despite the passage of centuries, Cato's life and teachings continue to resonate, offering timeless wisdom and inspiration.

CATO'S PHILOSOPHY AND ACTIONS

Cato's philosophy was not confined to intellectual contemplation but was intimately woven into his actions, in both his private life and his public role. As a Stoic, he held the firm belief that virtue was the highest good and that it should be pursued for its own sake. He upheld justice, courage, wisdom, and temperance - the four cardinal virtues of Stoicism - in all of his actions and decisions.

One of the defining moments of Cato's life that demonstrates his commitment to these principles was his uncompromising opposition to Julius Caesar. Cato saw in Caesar a threat to the Roman Republic's traditions and institutions, believing that his ambition for power would lead to tyranny. His resolute stance against Caesar was not a personal vendetta but rooted in his commitment to upholding justice and the rule of law. He championed the cause of the republic against the increasing centralization of power in the hands of a few individuals, a stance that eventually cost him his life.

Cato's pursuit of justice was not limited to grand political struggles; it was evident in his everyday actions as well. He was known for his integrity and his refusal to be swayed by bribes or personal gain. He was scrupulous in his dealings, insisting on paying the full price for a villa because he didn't want to exploit the seller's ignorance of its true value. His honesty was not a matter of convenience but a deeply ingrained principle that he upheld regardless of the circumstances.

Courage, another cardinal virtue, was also a defining characteristic of Cato's life. He showed remarkable bravery in the face of daunting challenges, both on the battlefield and in the political arena. His courage was not merely physical but moral as well. He was not afraid to stand alone in the Senate, advocating unpopular but principled positions, showing a fearless commitment to his beliefs.

Cato's wisdom, the third Stoic virtue, was evident in his deep understanding of Stoic philosophy and its application to life's complexities. His wisdom lay not in intellectual theorizing but in his capacity to navigate the challenging circumstances of his time with moral clarity and discernment. He saw the world for what it was, not what he wished it to be. This allowed him to act in accordance with reason and maintain his equanimity, even in the face of adversity.

The fourth virtue, temperance, was reflected in Cato's austere lifestyle. Despite coming from a privileged background, he chose to live simply, shunning the excesses and luxuries that many of his peers indulged in. His temperance was not merely a personal choice; it was a political statement, a rebuke of the decadence and moral corruption that he saw around him.

In interpreting Cato's actions through a Stoic lens, we see a man striving to live in accordance with nature and reason. He sought to act virtuously, irrespective of the outcomes. His focus was not on external rewards or recognition, but on performing his duty and maintaining his integrity. He understood, as the Stoics taught, that while we cannot control everything that happens to us, we can control how we respond. And his response, invariably, was to act with virtue.

Cato's life is a testament to the transformative power of Stoic philosophy. His philosophical beliefs were not abstract theories; they were guiding principles that shaped his actions and his character. His life provides a powerful example of Stoicism in action, showing how philosophical principles can guide us in confronting the challenges and moral dilemmas of our times.

In the modern world, where we often find ourselves facing ethical quandaries and complex challenges, Cato's example serves as a beacon, illuminating the path of virtue. His commitment to justice, courage, wisdom, and temperance, his unwavering adherence to principle, and his resilience in the face of adversity provide us with a blueprint for living a meaningful and virtuous life.

Cato's steadfast adherence to his beliefs was not without its critics. His unwavering consistency, while admirable, was also seen as rigid and inflexible. But from a Stoic perspective, this was not a flaw but rather a manifestation of his commitment to virtue and integrity. He saw no need for compromise when it came to upholding principles. To Cato, bending to the winds of convenience was a betrayal of his philosophical ideals.

In the political machinations of the Roman Senate, where alliances often shifted, and principles were frequently compromised for personal gain or political expediency, Cato's stand was seen as obstinate. Yet, it was this very quality that made him a beacon of integrity in an environment rife with corruption and opportunism. It is this aspect of his character that has ensured his legacy as one of the most principled political figures in history.

Cato's life also provides a vivid illustration of Stoic teachings on the nature of external things and our reactions to them. The Stoics taught that our judgments about external things – whether they are good or bad – lie within our control. Cato's actions reflect this teaching. He demonstrated an impressive ability to maintain his equanimity in the face of challenging situations, acting out of reason rather than emotion.

His death, a defiant act against the perceived tyranny of Julius Caesar, further exemplifies his philosophical beliefs. He chose to take his life rather than live under a regime he considered to be unjust. While this act is a subject of ethical debate, from a Stoic perspective, it represents the ultimate assertion of agency over one's life and an unwavering commitment to principle.

The concept of death, as understood by the Stoics, provides context to this act. Stoics regard life as a preferred indifferent, valuable but not at the expense of virtue. For Cato, living under what he saw as an unjust regime meant compromising his virtue. His suicide was a demonstration of his belief that life, while valuable, was not the ultimate good; virtue was.

Cato's life offers valuable insights for modern readers. In our increasingly complex world, where we are often faced with ethical dilemmas and conflicting interests, Cato's example serves as a reminder of the value of integrity, moral courage, and principled action. His story provides us with a concrete demonstration of Stoic philosophy in action and highlights the potential of these principles to guide us in navigating the challenges of modern life.

In conclusion, Cato's life was a testament to the transformative power of Stoic philosophy. His actions, driven by his commitment to virtue and principle, reflect the core tenets of Stoicism. They serve as a vivid reminder of the potential of Stoic philosophy to guide us in living a life of integrity, courage, and principled action, regardless of our circumstances. Cato's life, as I interpret it, invites us to reflect on our values and actions and challenges us to strive for virtue in our lives.

THE LEGACY OF CATO

Cato the Younger's life stands as a testament to Stoicism in action, leaving an enduring legacy that continues to influence and inspire those who follow Stoic philosophy. His unwavering commitment to virtue, his moral courage in the face of adversity, and his embodiment of Stoic principles in both private and public life have secured his place as a significant figure within the Stoic tradition.

Cato's influence extends far beyond the chronicles of ancient history. His life is a beacon, demonstrating the transformative power of Stoic philosophy. He remains a touchstone for those seeking to apply Stoic principles in their lives today, providing a blueprint for living a life of integrity and principle. His actions, driven by a commitment to virtue and justice, reflect the core tenets of Stoicism – the pursuit of virtue as the highest good, the differentiation between things within our control and those outside it, and the acceptance of fate with equanimity.

In the realm of political discourse and public service, Cato's legacy is particularly impactful. His refusal to compromise his principles for personal gain, even in the face of overwhelming opposition, offers an inspiring narrative for contemporary politicians and public figures. His life serves as a stark reminder that public service can be guided by virtue and integrity, with a steadfast commitment to the common good over personal or partisan interests.

Cato's influence is not limited to those interested in Stoicism or political history. His story has universal appeal, offering timeless lessons on personal resilience, moral courage, and the power of principled action. He embodies the concept that one's value is not determined by external circumstances, but by the quality of one's character and the integrity of one's actions.

Cato the Younger's legacy continues to resonate in the modern world. As a Stoic of action, his life serves as a guide for those who seek to navigate their lives with integrity, courage, and principled action, following the path of virtue laid down by the Stoics. His life and teachings stand as a reminder of the enduring relevance and practicality of Stoic philosophy, providing inspiration and guidance to Stoics and non-Stoics alike.

———

Cato the Younger's journey and steadfast adherence to Stoicism present us with a comprehensive exploration of Stoic philosophy in action. His life encapsulates the central principles of Stoicism—virtue as the ultimate good, control over one's actions and responses, acceptance of fate, and dedication to truth and justice. Cato's robust embodiment of these principles reinforces the Stoic idea that philosophical teachings aren't simply intellectual exercises; they are guideposts for living a meaningful and virtuous life.

As we reflect on Cato's life, it becomes evident that the core values he lived by—integrity, courage, resilience—are not relics of a distant past but enduring virtues relevant to the challenges of the contemporary world. His actions remind us that Stoicism is a philosophy of life, providing practical guidelines for facing adversities, making ethical decisions, and leading a life aligned with one's principles.

As we transition to the next chapter, we carry with us the lessons from Cato's life, a vivid testament to Stoicism in action, to further explore the Stoic philosophy and its impact on later figures and contemporary life.

CHAPTER 13
HIEROCLES - THE STOIC OF CONNECTION

Hierocles, a Stoic philosopher from the 2nd century AD, is a figure that might not be as widely known as other Stoics such as Epictetus, Marcus Aurelius, or Seneca. Nonetheless, his contributions to Stoic philosophy, particularly his concept of "concentric circles of concern," hold a significant place within this school of thought and have the potential to resonate deeply with contemporary readers seeking guidance from Stoic wisdom.

Despite the relative scarcity of his work – only fragments of his original writings have survived the passage of time – Hierocles's teachings continue to intrigue, inspire, and offer profound insights. The crux of his philosophy, captured in his theory of concentric circles, lays down a practical framework for social interaction, portraying how the self can relate harmoniously to family, friends, and wider communities. In a way, Hierocles brings forward an astute perspective on empathy and social solidarity, woven into the fabric of Stoicism.

Hierocles was more than just a theoretician; he was a practical philosopher. His philosophical views were not merely confined to scholarly debate; instead, they served as a blueprint for day-to-day living. His teachings underscore the Stoic commitment to virtue and provide a road map for living in accordance with nature, a key tenet of Stoic philosophy.

Moreover, Hierocles emphasized the significance of fulfilling our social duties and fostering mutual understanding and empathy amongst all individuals. These teachings, timeless in their wisdom, continue to hold relevance in modern times, striking chords with anyone seeking to navigate social complexities with grace and virtue.

The study of Hierocles's life and teachings, therefore, does not merely involve the exploration of historical Stoicism; it is an inquiry into perennially relevant themes of human connection, social responsibility, and personal growth. As we delve deeper into his life and philosophy in this chapter, we'll discover a Stoic who, in many ways, bridges the gap between ancient wisdom and contemporary societal issues, a Stoic philosopher truly connected to the human condition.

EARLY LIFE AND PATH TO STOICISM

Much of Hierocles's early life remains shrouded in mystery due to the dearth of surviving records. What we do know, however, is that he was born in the 2nd century AD, in a time when the Roman Empire was at its zenith, and Stoicism was one of the predominant philosophical schools. Given the limited information about his personal life, any attempt to sketch his early years and path to Stoicism would involve some degree of inference and speculation based on the historical and social context of his time.

As a young man, Hierocles would have been exposed to a cultural milieu rich with intellectual vigor. It was an era of great philosophers and philosophies, each vying for recognition and followers. The Roman Empire, with its sheer scale and diversity, provided fertile ground for the free flow of ideas. Hierocles was born into a world where Stoicism had not only found acceptance but was also practiced by the elites of society, including the emperor Marcus Aurelius himself.

Hierocles might have been introduced to Stoic philosophy through the prevalent educational system of the time, which valued rhetoric and philosophy. Stoicism, with its practical approach and ethical focus, was likely to have appealed to a young mind seeking answers to life's fundamental questions. As he delved deeper into the Stoic teachings, Hierocles would have discovered a philosophy that emphasized virtue, duty, and living in harmony with nature – principles that would resonate throughout his life and teachings.

Hierocles's path to Stoicism was likely a combination of intellectual curiosity, personal inclination towards the Stoic ideals of virtue and wisdom, and the influence of the socio-cultural environment of the Roman Empire. This journey towards Stoicism, however, was not just an intellectual pursuit for Hierocles. He embraced Stoicism as a way of life, and his philosophy was something he lived every day.

One can imagine that Hierocles's commitment to Stoicism was tested and strengthened through personal experiences and challenges. The Stoic emphasis on maintaining tranquility in the face of adversity, accepting the things beyond one's control, and focusing on personal virtue as the highest good – these teachings would have served as an invaluable guide as Hierocles navigated his life. They would have also shaped his interpretation of Stoicism and his contribution to the philosophy, particularly his concept of "concentric circles of concern."

Despite the lack of explicit records about Hierocles's early life, his dedication to Stoic philosophy, evident in the fragments of his work that have survived, suggests a deep and abiding engagement with these teachings. His path to Stoicism was perhaps less a choice and more a calling – a calling to explore and live by the principles of virtue, wisdom, and duty.

As we proceed further into the life and philosophy of Hierocles, we must remember that he was not just a philosopher but also a man who lived in challenging times. His teachings were both a reflection of his personal journey and a response to the social and cultural realities of his era. And within this context, Hierocles's Stoicism provides us with valuable insights into the application of this philosophy in daily life, offering timeless wisdom on managing personal relationships and social responsibilities.

HIEROCLES'S PHILOSOPHY AND TEACHINGS

Hierocles's philosophical contributions represent a significant part of Stoic literature and offer a unique perspective on interpersonal relationships within the Stoic framework. Perhaps his most memorable idea is that of the 'concentric circles of concern', a metaphor that encapsulates our relationships to the world and encourages us to draw those in outer circles closer to the center. This idea has implications that ripple through our understanding of empathy, compassion, and societal responsibility, while retaining the essence of Stoic thought about duty, virtue, and the interconnectedness of all beings.

Hierocles proposed that we imagine our place in the world as the center of a series of expanding circles. The first and closest circle represents our mind, the next encapsulates immediate family, followed by extended family, local community, countrymen, and finally, the entirety of the human race. This visualization served as a blueprint for the individual's moral duty and the exercise of virtue. As a Stoic, Hierocles encouraged us to 'draw in' the outer circles towards the center, thereby treating extended family as immediate family, local community as extended family, and so on. Through this, he articulated a Stoic form of 'ethical cosmopolitanism', where the individual extends love and concern to all humanity.

This model is not only a powerful representation of moral responsibility but also a practical guide to incorporating Stoic virtues in daily life. Stoicism, as you know, places a heavy emphasis on the cultivation and exercise of virtues – primarily wisdom, courage, justice, and temperance. Hierocles's circles provide a tangible way to practice these virtues, expanding the realm of our care and responsibility. As we 'draw in' the circles, we practice the virtue of justice, treating all individuals with fairness and kindness. We exercise wisdom by understanding our interconnectedness with the world. Courage is cultivated as we navigate the challenges that come with widened circles of concern, and temperance keeps our actions balanced and in check.

In historical context, Hierocles's philosophy presented a radical shift in thinking, promoting a worldview that transcended narrow tribalism and nationalism. His ideas were revolutionary for a time when societal structures were rigidly defined, and the 'other' was often seen with suspicion or hostility. His concept of 'ethical cosmopolitanism' could be seen as an antidote to the societal divisions and conflicts that characterized his era.

In my own experience, Hierocles's philosophy provides a powerful tool for cultivating empathy and expanding one's moral horizon. As we draw the outer circles closer, we realize that our actions affect not just ourselves or our immediate surroundings, but the world at large. This understanding can imbue our lives with a greater sense of purpose and responsibility. It also helps us recognize our shared humanity, fostering a spirit of cooperation, respect, and mutual care. The COVID-19 pandemic, for instance, has been a stark reminder of our interconnectedness and the need to extend our circles of concern.

Hierocles also taught us about 'oikeiosis', the Stoic doctrine of appropriation. Oikeiosis is the process by which we recognize what is truly 'our own'. For Stoics, the only thing truly belonging to us is our rational and moral capacity. Hierocles extended this idea, advocating that we should regard others' well-being as our own, echoing the broader theme of his philosophy of interconnectedness.

While Hierocles' philosophical works are fragmented and only partly preserved, we can still glean significant insights from what remains. Expanding on the model of concentric circles, he demonstrated the criticality of personal relationships in the practice of virtue. Each circle, according to him, necessitates different kinds of relationships – relationships of care, of respect, of understanding, and of collaboration. For example, relationships within the innermost circle (family) demand direct care and shared affection. In contrast, those in the outer circles, like fellow citizens or humankind, might involve respect, understanding, and a commitment to common welfare.

Hierocles also emphasized the role of philanthropy, or love for mankind, as part of Stoic practice. He taught that kindness, benevolence, and a sense of shared humanity should characterize our interactions with those in the outer circles. This extension of goodwill to all was a radical proposition, one that invited individuals to stretch their moral imagination and capabilities.

Examining Hierocles' philosophy through a historical lens, we can see it as an antidote to societal divisions of his time. Hierocles proposed a world in which familial ties, tribal loyalty, or regional affinity do not limit compassion and fairness. Instead, he advocated for an impartial, cosmopolitan love, regardless of nationality, ethnicity, or social standing. This was a radical and forward-thinking view, transcending the traditional boundaries of affiliation and care.

On a personal note, I've found Hierocles' philosophy profoundly impactful. In an era of increasing global interconnection and shared challenges like climate change, Hierocles's teachings remind us of our shared responsibility. His metaphorical circles have guided me to extend empathy and consideration to those beyond my immediate environment. This has influenced my personal and professional decisions, making me more aware of the broader implications of my actions and encouraging me to strive for fairness and equity in all dealings.

Moreover, Hierocles's concept of 'oikeiosis' has made me reevaluate my understanding of self-interest. Recognizing others' well-being as intricately linked to my own has fostered a deeper sense of compassion and solidarity in my interactions. This principle has profoundly shaped my perspective, teaching me that personal well-being and the collective good are not mutually exclusive, but interconnected and interdependent.

The relevance of Hierocles's philosophy in contemporary times is undeniable. Whether it's the global response to the COVID-19 pandemic, the fight against racial injustice, or efforts to combat climate change, Hierocles's teachings on expanded circles of concern and ethical cosmopolitanism are pertinent. They remind us of our collective duty to address global issues and of the importance of empathy and cooperation in doing so.

In sum, Hierocles's philosophy extends Stoicism into the social realm, emphasizing our duties to others and the importance of cultivating expansive, inclusive relationships. His teachings encourage us to practice virtue not only for personal growth but also for the betterment of our communities and the world at large. In a world increasingly fraught with division and conflict, Hierocles offers a path towards unity, mutual respect, and shared responsibility.

THE LEGACY OF HIEROCLES

The legacy of Hierocles is deep-rooted in the understanding and practice of modern Stoicism. It is not just in the realm of philosophical contemplation, but his teachings manifest in several aspects of contemporary life, education, and policymaking.

Hierocles' vision of concentric circles of concern remains one of the most relatable and compelling ethical frameworks within Stoic philosophy. His ideas have provided an accessible tool for people to understand the notion of 'oikeiosis' - the development of appropriate and beneficial relationships, each with its distinct degree of closeness and obligation. Hierocles' model promotes empathy, understanding, and social cohesion, values as much needed today as in his own time.

Modern-day Stoics often refer to Hierocles's circles as a guide to negotiate their interpersonal relationships and duties. They aspire to live up to his ideals, extending care from their immediate family to their wider community, and ultimately, to all of humanity. These concentric circles have become a blueprint for Stoic love, setting a bar for what it means to live a virtuous life.

Hierocles' ideas have also been embraced by the wider psychological and educational community. His concentric circles have been used as a teaching tool in character education programs to promote empathy and inclusivity. Even mental health professionals have utilized this model to aid clients in understanding and improving their relationships.

In terms of societal impact, Hierocles' concepts have been instrumental in shaping the ideals of cosmopolitanism. His philosophy underlies much of our contemporary discourse on global citizenship, collective responsibility, and international cooperation. The echoes of his teachings are found in our efforts towards global equity, be it in healthcare, education, or climate justice.

Overall, the legacy of Hierocles is not just confined to academic discussions on Stoicism but has permeated the fabric of our society. His teachings continue to resonate, offering us a framework to navigate our relationships, fulfill our social responsibilities, and contribute to a better, more compassionate world.

———

In understanding Hierocles and his teachings, we recognize the breadth and depth of Stoicism. His philosophy serves as a potent reminder that Stoicism is not only a guide for individual conduct, but also a philosophy advocating empathy, understanding, and social responsibility. Hierocles shows us that Stoicism encourages not just introspection, but also an outward expansion of care and concern, urging us to be mindful citizens of the world.

This understanding sets the stage for our exploration of our next Stoic philosopher, Gaius Musonius Rufus. Rufus, often referred to as "the Roman Socrates," further emphasizes the Stoic belief in virtue and action, focusing particularly on the practical application of Stoic principles in daily life. His life and teachings will provide us with further insights into how Stoicism can shape not only our personal decisions but also our social interactions and contributions to our communities.

CHAPTER 14
GAIUS MUSONIUS RUFUS - THE PRACTICAL STOIC

G aius Musonius Rufus, often known as "the Roman Socrates," held a place of high esteem among the Stoic philosophers of his era. Born in the first century AD in Volsinii, Italy, Rufus rose to prominence in a Rome that was rocked by political turmoil and social change. However, his strong moral compass and profound philosophical insights proved to be an oasis of wisdom and tranquility amid this tumultuous landscape.

Throughout his life, Rufus remained a steadfast proponent of Stoicism, a school of philosophy that posits that virtue, based on knowledge and reason, is the supreme good. Stoics, such as Rufus, advocate for an ascetic life where one must strive to control their responses to external circumstances and preserve their internal peace. However, Rufus's Stoicism was not merely about stern self discipline. It was a philosophy of action, deeply entrenched in the practical realities of life.

Rufus's contributions to Stoicism stand out for their applicability and relevance. He was a practical Stoic who believed in learning by doing. For him, philosophy was not merely a subject to be discussed and debated in the lecture halls but a guide for living a virtuous life.

He maintained that the teachings of philosophy should be manifested in one's everyday actions and interactions.

In Rufus's Stoicism, there was a strong emphasis on equality and social justice. He was one of the few philosophers of his time who argued that women were as capable of practicing philosophy and achieving virtue as men. These progressive views on gender equality resonate even in the present day, making him a Stoic philosopher well ahead of his times.

Despite enduring hardships, including being exiled twice from Rome due to his outspoken nature, Rufus never swerved from his philosophical path. Instead, he used these adversities as opportunities to deepen his understanding and practice of Stoicism, epitomizing the Stoic ideal of finding tranquility amidst chaos.

Rufus's teachings, unfortunately, are not preserved in their entirety. Most of what we know about him comes from the discourses and fragments recorded by his students. Yet, even from these fragments, it's evident that his philosophy had a tangible quality that encouraged not just contemplation, but action.

This chapter will delve into the life, philosophy, and legacy of Rufus, a practical Stoic whose teachings continue to inspire and guide individuals who seek to apply Stoicism in their day-to-day lives.

EARLY LIFE AND PATH TO STOICISM

The story of Gaius Musonius Rufus begins in Volsinii, a town in the heart of Italy, where he was born in the year AD 30 into a prominent family. The environment of his childhood was deeply influenced by the prevalent political and cultural climate. In this period, Rome was under the leadership of Emperor Augustus who sought to restore traditional Roman moral and civic values, a movement that was, in many ways, synchronous with the principles of Stoicism.

Rufus's early education likely came from private tutors, as was the custom of the time for families of his social standing. While specific details of his education remain scarce, it is plausible that he was introduced to the works of eminent Greek philosophers, including those of Zeno of Citium, the founder of Stoicism, and his successors. These philosophical teachings would have complemented the practical education in law, rhetoric, and politics he would have received as preparation for his future role as a civic leader.

As Rufus entered adulthood, the Roman Empire underwent significant changes. Emperor Augustus passed away, and a series of rulers of varying competence and integrity succeeded him. These rulers, including Tiberius, Caligula, and Claudius, navigated their reigns with degrees of paranoia, cruelty, and incompetence that led to growing disillusionment among the people.

During these tumultuous times, Rufus emerged as a prominent philosopher and teacher in Rome. Stoicism, with its emphasis on virtue and self-control, provided a refuge of sorts during these troubled times. Its teachings offered a way for individuals to find peace and happiness within themselves, irrespective of their external circumstances.

The principles of Stoicism appealed to Rufus. He embraced the philosophy not merely as a theoretical framework but as a guide to live by. For Rufus, the Stoic tenets of self-control, courage, justice, and wisdom were not just abstract concepts; they were virtues to be practiced daily.

His commitment to Stoicism was such that he did not shy away from voicing his criticism against the rulers of his time. He was twice exiled from Rome, first by Emperor Nero and then by Vespasian, for his outspokenness. However, these trials did not deter him. Instead, they presented opportunities to practically apply the teachings of Stoicism. He continued his philosophical discourses and teachings even during his exiles, drawing upon his experiences as a testament to the Stoic ideals of resilience and tranquility in the face of adversity.

His path to Stoicism was not a conventional scholarly pursuit, but rather, a journey carved by personal experiences and the political realities of his time. His practice of Stoicism was grounded in real-life situations, emphasizing that philosophy is not just about theoretical understanding, but also about practical implementation. In essence, Rufus's journey towards Stoicism was not just a path he chose, but also a path that was shaped by the turbulence of the era he lived in.

Rufus's immersion in Stoicism would have required an in-depth understanding of its core principles. Stoicism was founded on the belief that virtue is the highest form of good and that we should strive to cultivate four cardinal virtues: wisdom, courage, justice, and temperance. Additionally, it proposed that everything outside of our own actions and attitudes, which we have direct control over, is indifferent, neither good nor bad. For Rufus, these were not mere philosophical ideals, but practical guidelines for how one should live their life.

As he grew older and rose in stature within the Roman society, Rufus demonstrated an unwavering dedication to these Stoic principles. This commitment extended beyond his personal actions and attitudes; he was devoted to imparting these values to others as a teacher. His lessons transcended the boundaries of a traditional classroom. His life itself became a testament to the practical application of Stoic principles.

While his birth and upbringing in a prominent family might have put him on a path towards Stoicism, it was his personal experiences and observations of the world around him that truly shaped his understanding and practice of this philosophy. He lived in a time of political upheaval and societal change. The power dynamics within the Roman Empire were shifting, the old values were being questioned, and new ideas were taking shape. It was within this context that Rufus saw the value and need for Stoicism.

His life was marked by two notable periods of exile, first under Nero and then under Vespasian. These experiences could have been debilitating, but Rufus, instead, used them to demonstrate the power of Stoicism. He showed how one could maintain tranquility in the face of adversity, how external circumstances could not affect the inner peace of a true Stoic. These experiences further strengthened his belief in Stoicism and reaffirmed his commitment to living according to its principles.

His approach to Stoicism was not just theoretical; it was eminently practical. For Rufus, Stoicism was not just about understanding the nature of the universe or the human soul, it was about learning how to live a good and virtuous life. His lessons often revolved around practical issues like the value of work, the importance of discipline, the role of women in society, and the need for sexual restraint. He emphasized the application of philosophy to everyday life and the importance of action in accordance with Stoic principles.

The world around him, the changes he saw in the Roman Empire, the trials and tribulations he faced – all these elements shaped Rufus's path to Stoicism. They shaped his understanding of the philosophy and informed his approach to teaching it. They made him not just a scholar of Stoicism, but a practitioner, a living embodiment of its principles. In essence, Rufus's path to Stoicism was as much a product of his times as it was of his personal conviction and commitment to this philosophy.

The trajectory of Rufus's life took a significant turn when he was introduced to the works of renowned Stoic philosophers such as Zeno, Cleanthes, and Chrysippus. The principles these philosophers espoused resonated deeply with Rufus. The idea that our happiness does not depend on external circumstances but on our own inner attitudes and actions, the Stoic commitment to virtue as the highest good, the emphasis on rationality and logic – all of these tenets appealed to Rufus's intuitive understanding of life and the world.

As he delved deeper into the teachings of Stoicism, Rufus found a philosophical framework that not only made sense to him but also provided a practical guide for living a good life. He was drawn to the Stoic emphasis on self-control, the cultivation of virtue, the importance of rational judgment, and the notion of living in accordance with nature. He believed that these teachings could help individuals lead meaningful and fulfilled lives regardless of their circumstances.

Rufus's dedication to Stoicism was not a passive commitment. He actively sought to live according to its principles and encouraged others to do the same. He held regular lectures, wrote extensively on Stoic philosophy, and engaged in vigorous debates with his contemporaries. Through his teaching, he hoped to demonstrate the practical benefits of Stoicism and inspire others to embrace its principles.

His commitment to Stoicism was further strengthened by his personal experiences. His two periods of exile, first under Nero and then under Vespasian, were significant challenges that could have easily broken a lesser man. But Rufus, drawing strength from his Stoic beliefs, navigated these periods with grace and fortitude. His ability to maintain tranquility and equanimity in the face of adversity demonstrated the practical value of Stoicism. These experiences served to reinforce his faith in the philosophy and reaffirmed his commitment to its principles.

Rufus's contribution to Stoicism was not just in his personal adherence to its principles, but also in his influence on others. He was a mentor to Epictetus, who would go on to become one of the most celebrated Stoic philosophers. His teachings inspired many of his contemporaries and continue to influence Stoic philosophy to this day.

In summary, Rufus's path to Stoicism was a product of his personal conviction, his experiences, and the influence of the Stoic philosophers who came before him. He was not just a passive recipient of Stoic teachings; he actively engaged with them, sought to understand them deeply, and applied them in his daily life. His commitment to Stoicism was not just theoretical; it was deeply practical, borne out of a belief that Stoicism provided a valuable guide for living a good life.

RUFUS'S PHILOSOPHY AND TEACHINGS

Gaius Musonius Rufus is perhaps best known for his practical interpretation of Stoicism. Unlike other philosophers who focused heavily on theoretical concepts, Rufus believed that philosophy should be lived and practiced. He posited that Stoicism was more than just a theory about the nature of the world and the human place within it; it was a guide to leading a virtuous life. For Rufus, Stoicism was not a mere intellectual exercise but a deeply personal and practical commitment.

The core of Rufus's teaching was the idea of virtue. Like other Stoics, he believed that virtue was the highest good and that it should be the central aim of human life. He defined virtue as a kind of harmony with nature, where one's actions, emotions, and thoughts are in alignment with the rational order of the universe. But Rufus went beyond this theoretical conception of virtue. He argued that virtue was something that could be developed and cultivated through deliberate practice and effort.

One of Rufus's key teachings was that philosophy should be practical and applicable in everyday life. He believed that the true test of a philosopher was not in their ability to engage in abstract theorizing but in their capacity to apply philosophical principles in their daily lives. For Rufus, philosophy was not just a subject to be studied; it was a way of life to be lived.

He emphasized the importance of self-discipline and self-control. He argued that we have the power to control our responses to external events and that we should strive to maintain a state of tranquility regardless of our circumstances. This concept of inner tranquility, which Rufus referred to as "ataraxia," was a central tenet of his philosophy.

Rufus also emphasized the value of reason and rationality. He argued that reason was the highest faculty of human beings and that it should guide all our actions and decisions. He believed that by using our reason, we could understand the nature of the universe, discern what is truly good and valuable, and guide our actions accordingly.

Rufus's philosophy also extended to social and ethical issues. He believed in the inherent dignity and worth of all human beings, regardless of their social status, gender, or ethnicity. He argued for the equality of women and men, a radical idea in his time. He also advocated for the humane treatment of slaves, arguing that they were rational beings deserving of respect and dignity.

Rufus's teachings were not just theoretical; they were deeply practical. He advocated for a simple lifestyle, free from the pursuit of wealth and luxury. He believed that the pursuit of external goods often led to unhappiness and that true fulfillment came from the cultivation of virtue and the practice of reason.

Rufus's philosophy has left a lasting impact on Stoicism. His emphasis on the practical application of Stoic principles, his focus on virtue and reason, and his ethical teachings have all shaped the development of Stoic philosophy. His influence can be seen in the works of later Stoic philosophers such as Epictetus and Marcus Aurelius, and his teachings continue to inspire and guide Stoics today.

Rufus's teachings on virtue were deeply intertwined with his emphasis on action. Unlike other Stoics, Rufus did not view virtue as a static state of being but as an active process of becoming. He saw virtue as something that is practiced and embodied through our actions. In this regard, he significantly expanded the scope of Stoic virtue ethics.

Rufus believed that the purpose of philosophy was not merely to inform but to transform. He was convinced that philosophy should guide our conduct, shape our character, and influence our decision-making. He saw philosophical wisdom as the compass that directs us towards virtue and away from vice. This belief was reflected in his teachings, which often took the form of practical advice on how to live a virtuous life.

Rufus's philosophy was grounded in a deep sense of social responsibility. He believed that we all have a duty to contribute to the common good and to promote justice and fairness in society. He urged his students to be active participants in their communities and to use their philosophical wisdom to address social problems.

Rufus was known for his ethical teachings, which were often ahead of their time. He argued for gender equality, stating that women and men had the same capacity for virtue and should, therefore, receive the same education. He also called for the humane treatment of slaves, a stance that was radical in his time.

Rufus's philosophy also touched upon matters of personal conduct. He advocated for a simple, austere lifestyle, free from the pursuit of material wealth and sensual pleasure. He believed that a life of simplicity and moderation was more conducive to virtue and happiness than a life of luxury and indulgence.

Despite the practical focus of his teachings, Rufus did not neglect the theoretical aspects of Stoicism. He presented a sophisticated understanding of the Stoic doctrine of Nature and the role of reason in human life. He argued that by aligning ourselves with Nature and using our reason, we can achieve a state of inner peace and contentment, regardless of our external circumstances.

Rufus also delved into the psychology of emotions. He proposed that our emotional reactions are within our control and that by exercising our rational judgment, we can prevent negative emotions like anger, fear, and desire from disturbing our inner tranquility. This belief laid the groundwork for later Stoic theories of emotion.

While Rufus's teachings were firmly rooted in the Stoic tradition, he brought a unique perspective to Stoic philosophy. His focus on the practical application of Stoic principles, his expansion of Stoic virtue ethics, and his forward-thinking ethical teachings all contribute to his unique contribution to Stoic philosophy.

An exploration of Rufus's teachings would not be complete without considering his view on hardships. To Rufus, hardships were not mere obstacles but opportunities for growth and moral development. He believed that by facing our challenges with courage and resilience, we can strengthen our character and progress towards virtue. This perspective aligns with the Stoic idea of amor fati or the love of fate. It encourages us to accept whatever happens to us, not with resignation but with affirmation, viewing every event, whether good or bad, as a chance to practice virtue.

Furthermore, Rufus deeply considered the subject of endurance. Endurance to him wasn't just about stoically accepting circumstances; it was about understanding the purpose behind enduring challenges and pain. He argued that any hardship can be endured if it leads to a good end. This view of endurance, tied intrinsically with a sense of purpose, makes enduring hardships an act of reason and virtue.

On another front, Rufus was well known for his views on relationships and familial duties. He argued that good relationships are based on virtue and mutual respect. He believed in the importance of familial duties, the mutual responsibilities between parents and children, and between siblings. He advocated for marital fidelity and exhorted his students to treat their spouses with respect and affection.

Rufus's practical advice extended to daily routines as well. He suggested that one should not indulge in excessive sleep or food, as these were counterproductive to the practice of virtue. He also held the view that one should engage in physical exercise regularly as it is important for maintaining health, which he saw as a duty to oneself and society.

In terms of professional conduct, Rufus taught that one should perform their work diligently and honestly. He believed that a good

Stoic should lead by example and show others the virtue of their philosophy through their actions.

Importantly, Rufus's teachings are not just a list of prescriptions and prohibitions. They represent a holistic approach to life that intertwines our moral, social, and personal responsibilities. They remind us that Stoicism is not a theoretical discipline but a way of life, a philosophy to be lived and practiced.

Interpreting Rufus's teachings personally, they seem to embody the essence of what it means to live a Stoic life. Rufus emphasizes the integration of philosophy into every aspect of life, and his teachings provide practical guidelines on how to do so. His focus on virtue as something active and embodied, his views on social responsibility, gender equality, humane treatment of slaves, the importance of familial duties, and his ethical stance on personal conduct all resonate strongly with me. His work offers a comprehensive guide to living a good life, to enduring hardships with a sense of purpose, and to the relentless pursuit of virtue.

In the final analysis, Rufus's philosophy exemplifies the practical aspect of Stoicism. His teachings serve as a vivid reminder that Stoicism is not an abstract theory but a practical philosophy designed to guide us in our daily lives. Rufus's Stoicism is a philosophy of action, a philosophy of responsibility, a philosophy of resilience, and, above all, a philosophy of virtue.

THE LEGACY OF RUFUS

The impact of Gaius Musonius Rufus on Stoicism cannot be overstated. His practical approach to Stoic philosophy has had a lasting effect, continuing to influence modern understanding and practice of Stoicism. Rufus taught that philosophy was not a parlor trick or a school subject but a way of life. It's his emphasis on action and practice that makes his work accessible and inspiring for those grappling with the Stoic philosophy today.

He advocated for Stoic principles in a tangible, practical manner that people could incorporate into their daily lives. His teachings inspire individuals to practice Stoicism not just theoretically but practically. Rufus's emphasis on the need for continuous practice of virtue in everyday life is a vital aspect of his legacy. His practicality sets a clear path for those striving to live a Stoic life in the 21st century.

Rufus also stood out for his radical ideas about gender equality, asserting that women are just as capable of practicing Stoicism and virtue as men. This belief remains a significant part of his legacy, bringing a fresh perspective to the understanding of ancient Stoicism and making it a progressive philosophy, even in today's context.

Rufus's belief in the inherent ability of every human being, regardless of their status or background, to achieve virtue through their actions also resonates deeply in a modern context. He argued that everyone had the capacity for virtue and wisdom, a belief that democratized philosophy and made it accessible to all.

In the landscape of Stoic philosophy, Rufus's teachings continue to be a beacon for those seeking a practical way to navigate their lives. They continue to inspire, providing a road map to a virtuous life that can weather all of life's adversities. His teachings, firmly rooted in the reality of daily life, have transcended centuries and continue to resonate in the heart of the Stoic philosophy.

In conclusion, Gaius Musonius Rufus's legacy lies not only in his contribution to Stoic philosophy but also in the timeless relevance of his teachings. Through his practical approach to Stoicism and his unique insights into virtue, equality, and wisdom, Rufus remains a vital figure in the exploration and practice of Stoicism today and for the generations to come.

––––––––

The life and teachings of Gaius Musonius Rufus remain a fundamental cornerstone for understanding Stoicism in its most practical form. Rufus emphasized the daily practice of philosophy, a philosophy of action and deed, not just of thought. His pragmatic approach resonates deeply with those who seek a comprehensive and actionable guide in the Stoic way of life.

Through his teachings, Rufus demonstrated the transformative power of Stoicism. He advocated the cultivation of virtues such as self-control, courage, justice, and wisdom, using everyday experiences as a training ground. His insistence on applying philosophy to daily life made Stoicism an accessible and useful tool for navigating the complexities and challenges of existence.

Rufus's views on equality were radical for his time and have cemented his legacy as a progressive Stoic. His belief that women were equally capable of practicing philosophy and virtue challenges the conventional view of ancient Stoicism and adds a refreshing perspective to our understanding of it.

The practical Stoicism of Rufus is deeply relevant today as we navigate an increasingly complex world. It is a reminder that philosophy should not be confined to scholarly discourse but should be lived and practiced in our day-to-day lives. The lessons of Rufus provide valuable insights into leading a virtuous life and finding tranquility amid adversity.

In conclusion, the life and teachings of Gaius Musonius Rufus serve as an invaluable resource for those interested in Stoicism. His focus on action and the application of Stoic principles to daily life render his teachings timeless and universally applicable.

CHAPTER 15
APPLYING STOICISM IN EVERYDAY LIFE

As we navigate through arguably the most significant chapter of our journey, we are about to embark on a task of amalgamating all the pearls of wisdom that we have collected from the lives and teachings of the great Stoic philosophers. This chapter, "Applying Stoicism in Everyday Life", stands as a bridge between the philosophical realm and our daily existence. It serves as an endeavor to translate the profound teachings of Stoicism into actionable steps, enabling us to lead a more resilient, tranquil, and purposeful life.

In the preceding chapters, we have dwelled deep into the labyrinth of Stoicism, unearthing its roots, tracing its evolution, and understanding its principles as preached and practiced by its proponents like Marcus Aurelius, Seneca, Epictetus, and others. We have deciphered how Stoicism equips us with a unique perspective towards life, teaching us to differentiate between things within our control and those beyond, urging us to embrace our fate with grace, and enabling us to maintain equanimity in the face of adversities.

In this chapter, we are going to bring Stoicism out of the annals of ancient texts and into the beating heart of our present lives. We will be sharing personal anecdotes and stories, narrating experiences where Stoic principles helped in overcoming adversities and achieving tranquility. A step-by-step guide will follow these stories, providing clear, actionable steps to incorporate Stoic practices into your daily routines. Whether you are a beginner or well-acquainted with Stoic principles, this guide will serve as a tool to further your understanding and application.

We will also have specific reflection points to help you analyze your progress, modify your approach, and gauge your understanding. These reflective exercises will ensure that you are not merely a passive recipient of knowledge, but an active participant in your journey towards Stoic wisdom. They will prompt you to engage with the content, to question, comprehend, and internalize the teachings.

Furthermore, the chapter will continuously tie back the concepts to their respective philosophers, keeping the teachings rooted in their historical context and reinforcing your understanding of the original texts. These tie-backs will help you to connect the principles with the philosophers, thereby enriching your holistic understanding of Stoicism.

Lastly, the chapter will challenge you to push your boundaries, to step out of your comfort zone, and to put the Stoic principles to test through actionable challenges. These challenges are not meant to intimidate you but to inspire you, to stimulate your intellectual curiosity, and to fuel your personal growth.

As we unravel this chapter, remember that embracing Stoicism is not about overnight transformation but about patient and persistent practice. It is a journey, not a destination. It is about gradual but genuine change. As we navigate through this chapter, let us apply Stoicism in our lives, not merely as a philosophy but as a way of life.

———

As I reflect on my own life, the stoic teachings have time and again served as a guiding light in the face of adversity. There's one story in particular that stands out and demonstrates the application of these principles during trying times.

It was during a period when I was at the pinnacle of my career. The joy of professional success was exhilarating, and it seemed like life couldn't get any better. But as Heraclitus, an early philosopher who influenced Stoicism, rightly said, "Character is destiny." Unforeseen circumstances soon tested my character to its limits.

I was heading a major project at work. It was a massive responsibility with substantial investments and the expectations were sky-high. However, due to some unexpected market downturns and project complications, the initiative began facing significant difficulties. The threat of failure loomed large, and with it, the fear of substantial financial losses and the associated blame and career repercussions.

The situation was grim, and there seemed to be no light at the end of the tunnel. I could feel the weight of despair sinking in, bringing with it anxiety, fear, and a sense of impending doom. The relentless stress was all-consuming, and my peace of mind was in shambles.

It was during these troubled times that I found solace in Stoicism. I turned to the teachings of Epictetus, who made a clear distinction between things that are within our control and those that are not. He said, "Some things are in our control and others not. Things in our control are opinion, pursuit, desire, aversion, and, in a word, whatever are our own actions. Things not in our control are body, property, reputation, command, and, in one word, whatever are not our own actions."

I realized I was burdening myself with worry over factors beyond my control: the market trends, the actions of competitors, and the financial repercussions. This worry was futile, serving no practical purpose, and only enhancing my distress.

What I could control, however, were my actions and responses. I could work diligently, coordinate with my team efficiently, and make informed decisions. I could choose not to let the fear of potential failure prevent me from giving my best. I could accept that failure, if it came, would be a situation to handle, not an insurmountable disaster.

This stoic understanding brought about a massive shift in my perspective. I shifted focus from my fears to my actions. Despite the challenging circumstances, I worked with renewed zeal and determination, no longer paralyzed by what could go wrong.

In the end, although the project did not achieve the desired success, it was not a complete failure. There were losses, but they were manageable. There were lessons learned, improvements identified, and strategies evolved. But most importantly, I maintained my tranquility and resilience, successfully navigating through a storm that could have wreaked havoc on my peace of mind.

My experience underlines the essence of Marcus Aurelius's words, "You have power over your mind - not outside events. Realize this, and you will find strength."

While the tale of professional adversity provides insight into Stoicism's value in navigating tumultuous times, it is equally significant to explore how it contributes to an enduring state of tranquility and contentment. My journey to finding this tranquility was paved with a series of conscious decisions and incremental lifestyle changes.

I was in the prime of my adulthood when I found myself frequently stressed and dissatisfied. My job was demanding, relationships were complex, and societal pressures were omnipresent. I felt like I was chasing after a perpetually moving target of fulfillment and contentment. No matter how much I achieved or how hard I worked, the tranquility I sought seemed elusive.

Enter Stoicism.

One day, I stumbled upon a quote from Seneca: "True happiness is... to enjoy the present, without anxious dependence upon the future." This simple statement resonated deeply within me. I was so engrossed in fretting over the future and dwelling on the past that I was missing out on the beauty of the present. It was as if I was watching my life pass by while I stood on the sidelines, entangled in a web of concerns and expectations.

I realized that I had the power to change this. Stoicism, with its emphasis on mindfulness and acceptance, provided a roadmap. I decided to make a conscious effort to live more in the present and appreciate the simple joys that each day brings.

One practical step I took was to incorporate mindfulness into my daily routine. I began with a simple practice of observing my thoughts and emotions without judgment during quiet moments of the day. Over time, I extended this mindfulness to other activities - eating, walking, and even mundane chores. This practice was not easy, and there were numerous occasions when I found myself slipping back into old habits of worry and distraction. But, like a gentle observer, I would acknowledge the lapse and guide my mind back to the present.

I also made an effort to incorporate gratitude into my daily life. Each night before sleep, I would reflect on my day and list three things I was grateful for. Some days, the list comprised simple pleasures like a good meal or a warm sunset, while other days it included deeper aspects such as a loved one's health or a personal achievement. This ritual of daily gratitude significantly shifted my focus from what I lacked to what I possessed, creating a sense of contentment and abundance.

The transformation did not happen overnight, and it required consistent effort and commitment. But as days turned into months, I began noticing a change. My mind was less cluttered, my heart more at peace. I was more aware of my thoughts and reactions, and I found myself better equipped to handle stress and disappointments. I found joy in the simplest of things, like a cup of morning coffee, a book, or a walk in the park. In essence, I found the tranquility I had been seeking.

The journey to achieving tranquility is a deeply personal and ongoing one, but Stoicism provides an invaluable compass. As Marcus Aurelius said, "Very little is needed to make a happy life; it is all within yourself, in your way of thinking."

STEP-BY-STEP GUIDANCE

1. Embracing Amor Fati

Amor Fati, translated as "love of fate," is a central tenet of Stoic philosophy. It is a practice of embracing everything that life presents us, good or bad, as necessary and beneficial for our growth. By loving our fate, we acknowledge the natural flow of life and train ourselves to remain unperturbed by situations that are beyond our control.

One of the first steps towards embodying this Stoic concept was to identify instances where I struggled with acceptance. It could be something as minor as a traffic jam or as significant as a professional setback. I observed my reactions, my internal monologue, the resistance, and discomfort. I noticed the tension between reality and my expectations.

Next, I started to consciously alter my response in these situations. Instead of resistance, I would remind myself of Amor Fati. I would repeat to myself, "This is what the universe has presented me with, and I choose to accept and love it." It was challenging initially, but with persistence, it gradually started becoming more natural.

There was a shift in perspective over time. I saw how this acceptance didn't mean passivity, but it empowered me to respond effectively. If I was stuck in traffic, instead of fretting over the delay, I started to use the time to listen to an audiobook. If there was a professional setback, instead of dwelling on it, I took it as feedback and an opportunity to learn and improve.

The practice of Amor Fati is not about denying emotions or problems. It's about acceptance, learning from every situation, and using everything as a stepping stone towards growth and wisdom.

2. Practicing Negative Visualization

Negative visualization is another powerful Stoic practice. It involves visualizing negative scenarios or losses to appreciate what we have and mitigate the impact of potential negative events. Contrary to pessimism, it's a tool to increase our everyday contentment and prepare us mentally for life's challenges.

My first encounter with negative visualization was admittedly unsettling. Imagining losing loved ones, getting fired from a job, or facing health issues wasn't comforting. However, as I continued the practice, I realized its profound impact.

Visualizing loss reminded me of the impermanent nature of all things. It spurred gratitude for what I had in the present - a healthy body, a job, relationships, simple daily conveniences. This constant reminder led me to not take these things for granted and fostered a deep sense of appreciation and fulfillment.

In a practical sense, I would take out a few minutes every day for this practice. I would find a quiet place, close my eyes, and visualize a scenario where I had lost something or someone valuable. After the visualization, I would open my eyes and experience the relief of realizing that what I had imagined had not occurred and feel gratitude for what I still had.

Negative visualization also provided a safe space to explore fears and uncertainties. By mentally navigating through these scenarios, I felt more prepared to handle them if they were to occur in reality.

3. Implementing Dichotomy of Control

The Dichotomy of Control is a fundamental Stoic principle that instructs us to differentiate between things within our control and those beyond it. It encourages focusing our efforts on what we can control, like our thoughts, attitudes, and actions, and accepting what we can't, like the actions of others, the past, and most external events.

In my own life, I found this tenet incredibly freeing. I noticed how often my peace was disturbed by things beyond my control. A delayed flight, an unexpected rain, a friend running late, a colleague's rude remark, all caused unnecessary stress.

I began incorporating the Dichotomy of Control by consciously reminding myself of what was in my control in any given situation. When a flight was delayed, instead of fretting over it, I reminded myself that I had no control over it and focused instead on how I could utilize the extra time productively. This change in perspective eliminated a lot of unnecessary stress and anxiety.

But the most profound shift happened in my interactions with others. Previously, I would be bothered by others' opinions or actions, but once I understood that their actions were not within my control, it became easier to let go. I started focusing on my response, my attitude, and my behavior. This didn't mean that I became indifferent, but I learned to express my concerns without getting emotionally invested in the outcomes.

4. Applying the View from Above

The 'View from Above' is a Stoic meditative exercise where you visualize yourself from an external perspective, gradually zooming out to perceive a broader picture. This practice brings into focus the triviality of our daily worries in the grand scheme of things.

When I first tried this technique, I found it mentally challenging but very illuminating. Visualizing myself in the third person, then seeing myself from the room, the building, the city, the earth, and finally the vast cosmos, it gave me an almost humbling perspective.

The everyday issues, the stressors that seemed so significant, suddenly appeared minor. A work deadline, a disagreement with a friend, traffic congestion - all seemed incredibly small when viewed from the cosmic perspective.

The practice doesn't diminish personal experiences or problems but gives a refreshing viewpoint that fosters patience, tolerance, and resilience. It's a reminder of our small but integral part in the cosmic play and reinforces the interconnectedness of everything.

I found the View from Above technique particularly helpful during stressful situations. If I found myself overwhelmed or overreacting, I would take a few moments for this visualization. The resulting shift in perspective helped in calming down and approaching the situation with renewed patience and understanding.

REFLECTION POINTS

1. Reflecting on Adversity

Reflecting on adversity is an essential part of applying Stoicism in everyday life. It can help us turn challenges into opportunities for growth and wisdom. This does not mean we seek out hardship. Rather, we accept it as part of the human experience and use it to strengthen our character.

Reflecting on adversity has been a cornerstone of my own Stoic practice. During challenging times, I would pause and ask myself: "What is within my control?" This simple question helped distinguish between what I could and couldn't change, reducing unnecessary anxiety and allowing for more constructive responses.

Such reflections also encouraged a shift in perspective. Instead of seeing adversity as a stumbling block, I began to view it as a stepping stone towards becoming a wiser, more resilient individual. This mindset reframed obstacles as opportunities, enabling me to cope with adversity more effectively.

In your Stoic practice, remember that adversity is not inherently bad. Rather, it is our perception and reaction to it that determines its impact. By reflecting on adversity, we can cultivate resilience, embrace acceptance, and grow from our experiences.

2. Reflecting on Tranquility

Tranquility, or inner peace, is a coveted state of mind in Stoic philosophy. It is not merely the absence of turmoil but the presence of equanimity, regardless of life's ups and downs. This profound sense of serenity allows us to maintain our composure and clarity, even amidst chaos.

In my Stoic journey, reflecting on tranquility has been transformative. I found tranquility not by avoiding difficulties, but by learning to respond to them in more measured, thoughtful ways. By focusing on what's within my control and accepting what's not, I began to experience a sense of tranquility that felt both empowering and calming.

Moreover, tranquility became a form of resilience, an anchor in stormy seas. It didn't mean that I stopped feeling emotions or ignored pain. Instead, it provided a space where I could process these feelings without being consumed by them.

As you reflect on tranquility in your life, remember that it's not about achieving a constant state of calm. It's about cultivating the ability to return to that calm, no matter the circumstances. This, indeed, is the ultimate manifestation of Stoic tranquility.

3. Reflecting on Perspective

In Stoicism, 'the view from above' is a powerful mental exercise that allows us to gain a different perspective on our lives and situations. It involves visualizing ourselves from a bird's eye view, and then progressively expanding that view to include our surroundings, our city, our planet, and even our universe. This exercise helps us realize our relative insignificance in the grand scheme of things, and it's designed to alleviate our anxieties and worries, which often arise from overemphasis on self.

On a personal level, this tool has brought a sense of calm and tranquility to my life. In moments of heightened stress or frustration, I have frequently used this technique to reorient my perspective, reminding myself of the broader picture.

I encourage you to reflect on times when you've had a change of perspective. How did it impact your emotions and actions? Are there instances in your life now where a shift in perspective might be beneficial? Use these reflection points as tools to integrate the 'view from above' into your daily life, enhancing your capacity to deal with life's ups and downs with serenity and wisdom.

TIE-BACKS TO PHILOSOPHERS

1. Marcus Aurelius

Marcus Aurelius, often hailed as the philosopher king, stands as an enduring figure of Stoic philosophy. His personal writings, collected in "Meditations," offer profound insights on resilience, virtue, and the nature of human life. Reading his meditations, one can't help but feel a deep sense of connection with this ancient Roman emperor, who, despite his position and power, faced similar struggles as we do and turned to Stoicism for guidance.

I have often found solace and direction in Marcus's words during moments of turmoil or indecision. His reflections provide a direct line to the Stoic teachings that tell us to focus only on what is within our control and to accept the rest with equanimity. One of his most profound ideas that I often return to is: "You have power over your mind - not outside events. Realize this, and you will find strength."

Now, let's tie this back to the practical strategies we've discussed. In the context of embracing amor fati, Marcus Aurelius is a guiding light. His meditations reveal a man who deeply understood and accepted the impermanent and unpredictable nature of life. He consistently emphasized the necessity to accept and even love our fate.

Consider your approach to the struggles you face. How can you implement Marcus's teachings into your responses to adversity? Are there aspects of your life where you are resisting what is, rather than accepting and working with it? Marcus Aurelius serves as a powerful reminder that our power lies not in changing the world to our will, but in adjusting our will to the world.

2. Seneca

Seneca, a prominent Stoic philosopher and statesman, is renowned for his profound letters and essays that delve into the human condition. His teachings were instrumental in shaping my understanding and practice of Stoic philosophy. His ideas, although written nearly two millennia ago, remain strikingly relevant and practical in today's world.

Seneca's letters often encapsulate the core values of Stoic philosophy, including the concept of 'tranquillitas,' a state of inner tranquility and composure regardless of external circumstances. His words act as a powerful reminder that the goal of Stoicism isn't to suppress or avoid emotions but to approach them rationally and calmly. In the tumultuous storm of life, Seneca instructs us to find a serene harbor within ourselves.

When we discuss the practice of Negative Visualization, Seneca comes to the fore. He instructed us to periodically meditate on potential losses or hardships. "We suffer more often in imagination than in reality," he wrote. But Seneca did not intend for us to dwell on these negative thoughts. Instead, he proposed this exercise to foster resilience and reduce anxiety about potential misfortunes.

Let's think about the practical applications of this wisdom. When we reflect on potential challenges or losses, we become better equipped to handle them if they occur. More importantly, we learn to appreciate what we have now, fostering a sense of gratitude for the present moment. Seneca's wisdom reminds us that we can navigate life's challenges with a calm mind, resilience, and the awareness that happiness is rooted in our reactions, not in external events.

3. Epictetus

Epictetus, a slave turned Stoic philosopher, had a profound influence on my understanding of Stoicism and its practical applications. Born into hardship, he demonstrated that external conditions need not dictate our internal state of being. His teachings strike at the heart of Stoic philosophy, emphasizing that our responses to events, rather than the events themselves, determine our peace and happiness.

Epictetus is perhaps best known for his concept of the 'Dichotomy of Control,' a central tenet of Stoic philosophy. He proposed that some things are within our control—our judgments, impulses, desires, aversions—while others are not—external events, other people's actions, or our own bodies. Recognizing this division and focusing our efforts on what we can control is essential to maintaining tranquility and reducing unnecessary suffering.

Reflect on this teaching and its practical implications. When faced with adversity, we can find solace in knowing that we have control over our responses, our interpretations, and our attitudes. When we truly internalize this understanding, we can meet any challenge head-on, knowing that our tranquility is secure within us, untouched by external disturbances.

Epictetus also emphasized the importance of discipline, reason, and virtue. He saw virtue not as an abstract idea but as a guide to life's daily actions. He taught that we should lead our lives according to reason, aligning our actions with our values, and consistently striving for virtue.

As we navigate the ebbs and flows of life, we can always draw upon the wisdom of Epictetus. His teachings remind us that we have the power to maintain our tranquility, to respond to events with reason, and to lead a life guided by virtue.

ACTIONABLE CHALLENGES

Challenge 1: Embrace Amor Fati

For the first challenge, I invite you to embrace the principle of Amor Fati, the love of fate. This principle encourages us to not only accept, but actively appreciate everything that happens to us, treating each event as something that was meant to happen.

Start with small inconveniences, such as a traffic jam or a delayed flight. Instead of allowing frustration to settle, view these situations as opportunities for growth and learning. Perhaps the traffic jam grants you extra time to listen to an audiobook or the delayed flight allows you to catch up on some reading.

Extend this practice to larger events in your life. Maybe you didn't get the job you wanted, or a relationship ended. Accept these as part of your journey and find ways to appreciate them. The job rejection can be an impetus to improve your skills, the end of a relationship can be a chance to rediscover your own worth and identity.

Remember, the aim is not to suppress negative feelings but to reinterpret the situation and find the silver lining. It might be difficult initially, but with consistent practice, you'll find yourself becoming more resilient and calm in the face of adversity.

Challenge 2: Practicing Negative Visualization

For the second challenge, we'll delve into the art of Negative Visualization. It might sound counterintuitive, even pessimistic, but it's quite the opposite. It's a powerful tool that the Stoics used to foster gratitude and prevent hedonic adaptation - the tendency to quickly return to a baseline level of satisfaction no matter what happens in life.

To practice Negative Visualization, carve out a few moments each day to reflect on the transience of life and the impermanence of all that we hold dear. This is not an invitation to dwell in sadness or fear, but a way to appreciate the present moment and the things we often take for granted.

Imagine, for instance, losing something you value: a beloved pet, your job, or even a talent you have. Reflect on how it would feel if these were taken away from you. Doing so should not provoke anxiety, but rather, foster an increased appreciation for these aspects of your life while they are still present.

This practice can make you more mindful of your blessings, helping you to relish them more deeply and anxiously cling to them less.

Challenge 3: Implementing the Dichotomy of Control

The third challenge involves the understanding and application of the Dichotomy of Control. This Stoic principle, beautifully articulated by Epictetus, calls for discerning what is within our control from what is not. It's a simple yet profound concept that can be remarkably liberating once fully grasped and applied.

For this challenge, take a moment to examine the concerns and anxieties that currently occupy your mind. Make a list of these worries and then, one by one, decide whether they fall into the category of things within your control or things outside of it.

For issues that are within your control, formulate an action plan to address them. For those outside your control, try to let go and accept them as they are, knowing that worrying won't change the outcome.

Understanding and applying the Dichotomy of Control helps us direct our energy and attention towards actions that can truly make a difference in our lives, while simultaneously cultivating a sense of peace and acceptance towards those things we can't change.

Challenge 4: Applying the View from Above

The final challenge is to practice the 'View from Above,' a meditative exercise that Marcus Aurelius often referenced in his writings. The idea here is to step back from our immediate circumstances and adopt a more universal perspective.

The 'View from Above' can start simply. Find a quiet space where you can sit comfortably and undisturbed. Close your eyes and imagine you are slowly ascending, leaving your physical location. Continue this ascension, seeing your town, then your country, and finally, the Earth from space.

From this vantage point, the stresses and anxieties that once seemed so significant might now appear trivial against the grand backdrop of the universe. Similarly, our joys and successes are also humbled, reminding us to keep a level head in times of happiness.

Remember to carry out this exercise whenever you feel overwhelmed or elated. Regular practice will allow you to quickly and effectively gain perspective, leading to a more balanced and stoic response to life's ups and downs.

———

In this chapter, we delved deep into the practical application of Stoicism in our everyday lives. We shared personal anecdotes, learned step-by-step techniques, pondered upon reflection points, revisited the insights of the great Stoic philosophers, and challenged ourselves with actionable tasks.

Each element was designed to guide you to internalize the core principles of Stoicism and allow its wisdom to permeate your thoughts, actions, and reactions. Remember, Stoicism is not a destination, but a journey. It is a continuous practice of shaping our character, understanding, and responses to the world. So, take a deep breath and step forward with courage and serenity on the path to a more Stoic life.

CHAPTER 16
THE CONTINUOUS JOURNEY

Stoicism, as we have discovered through the pages of this book, is far from being a quick-fix solution or a short-term endeavour. It is a continuous journey that requires a lifelong commitment and a deliberate, conscious choice to live a certain way. It demands consistent practice and a readiness to learn, unlearn, and adapt.

I want to re-emphasize the fact that Stoicism is not about achieving perfection. It's not about reaching a place where we are immune to life's challenges or invincible in the face of adversity. No, it's about cultivating a mindset that allows us to navigate life with resilience, wisdom, and a sense of tranquility. It's about learning to control our reactions, recognizing the transient nature of our emotions and experiences, and discerning between what we can control and what we must let go.

As someone who has embarked on this journey, I can assure you that the path of Stoicism is not a linear one. It's marked by setbacks, stumbling blocks, and periods of self-doubt. Yet, each of these experiences has served as an opportunity to deepen my understanding of this ancient philosophy and its relevance in today's world.

There have been times when I felt that I had failed as a Stoic.

Instances when I reacted impulsively to provocation, allowed fear or worry to cloud my judgment, or simply found it hard to embrace amor fati. However, over time, I have realized that these moments of 'failure' are indeed an integral part of this journey. They serve as potent reminders of our human tendency to falter and our capacity to learn, adapt, and grow.

One of the key breakthroughs in my journey came when I realized that the practice of Stoicism isn't confined to meditation sessions or journaling exercises. Instead, it extends to every moment of our lives - how we engage with others, how we respond to unexpected events, how we handle stress, and even how we view ourselves. Stoicism, at its core, is about transforming the way we live and interact with the world.

A significant part of my journey also involved understanding that Stoicism isn't a philosophy of isolation or emotional suppression. The Stoics didn't advocate turning away from society or suppressing our feelings. Instead, they urged us to engage fully with life while maintaining an equanimous mind, to acknowledge our emotions without being overwhelmed by them.

The beauty of Stoicism lies in its simplicity and its universal applicability. Whether you're a student, a professional, a parent, or a retiree - Stoicism has something to offer everyone. Its principles can be applied in the office, at home, in our relationships, and most importantly, in our relationship with ourselves.

As I reflect on my own Stoic journey, I am reminded of the wisdom of Marcus Aurelius: "The art of life is more like the wrestler's art than the dancer's, in respect of this, that it should stand ready and firm to meet onsets which are sudden and unexpected." These words ring true to my experiences. Life is full of unexpected challenges, sudden twists, and turns, but adopting Stoicism has given me a robust framework to face these challenges head-on.

This book, as I stated in the introduction, is not a work by a perfect Stoic. Instead, it is a collection of my insights, interpretations, and experiences as someone who strives to practice Stoicism each day. I do not profess to have all the answers or solutions, but I genuinely believe that the principles of Stoicism can help us navigate the complexities of modern life with greater serenity, resilience, and wisdom.

As we come to the close of this book, I want to encourage each one of you embarking on your own Stoic journey. Remember, it's okay to stumble and fall. It's okay to experience doubt and confusion. The essence of Stoicism lies not in perfect adherence to its principles but in our willingness to strive, learn, and grow.

The Stoic path, much like life itself, is a continuous journey rather than a destination. As you go forward, let the wisdom of the ancient Stoics guide you, let their teachings inspire you, and let their resilience fortify you.

In closing, I want to leave you with the words of Seneca, "As long as you live, keep learning how to live." Embrace this philosophy, nurture your curiosity, and commit to lifelong learning. The road ahead may be long and winding, but remember, every step taken in wisdom is a step closer to tranquility and resilience.

CHAPTER 17
INVITING YOU ON THE JOURNEY

As we come to the end of this book, it is important to remember that the Stoic journey is not a solitary one. Just as I have extended an invitation to you to explore this ancient philosophy, I also encourage you to invite others. Share the teachings, share your experiences, and engage in dialogues about Stoicism. We grow not just by learning, but also by teaching and discussing.

Let me share a bit more about why it is essential for all of us to embark on this journey. In our ever-changing and fast-paced world, finding an anchor, a philosophy that helps us stay balanced and resilient, is crucial. That is what Stoicism has done for me. It has given me a perspective to approach life with serenity, courage, and wisdom.

I sincerely hope that this book has provided you with insights, sparked your curiosity, and perhaps kindled an interest in Stoicism. I hope it has shown you that Stoicism isn't a dry, academic philosophy, but a vibrant and practical guide to living well.

As you read the last few lines of this book, consider this not as an ending, but as a beginning. A beginning of a journey that will be filled with introspection, growth, and transformation. And though it might be challenging, remember that, in the wise words of Marcus Aurelius, "The obstacle is the way."

If there is one thing that I would like you to remember from this book, it is this: Stoicism is a practical philosophy that is meant to be lived, not just learned. So, as you step into the world after reading this book, I invite you to embody the Stoic principles in your daily life.

Remember, being a Stoic is not about suppressing emotions or detaching from the world, rather it is about embracing life as it comes with an equanimous mind. A Stoic finds solace not in external validations or possessions but in their own virtue and character. They are grounded in the present moment, resilient in the face of adversity, and always willing to learn and grow.

In the spirit of the Stoic philosophy of lifelong learning, let this book not be your last stop but a stepping stone in your exploration of Stoicism. There are numerous resources out there - books, online courses, communities, and seminars that offer a wealth of knowledge about Stoicism.

Before I sign off, I want to thank you for being a part of my Stoic journey. By reading this book, you have shared in my exploration and interpretation of Stoicism, and for that, I am truly grateful. I wish you all the best on your Stoic journey and may you find the tranquility, resilience, and wisdom that you seek.

And so, my fellow journeyers, until our paths cross again, I bid you farewell and good luck on your journey.

AFTERWORD

As I come to the end of this book, I want to express my gratitude for joining me on this Stoic journey. Stoicism: A Timeless Path to Inner Peace has been a labor of love, blending ancient wisdom with personal experiences.

My aim was to provide a guide—a compass to navigate life's challenges, cultivate resilience, and discover inner peace. Stoicism offers practical teachings for embracing virtue and finding tranquility.

I encourage you to continue exploring Stoic philosophy. Delve into the works of Marcus Aurelius, Epictetus, Seneca, and other Stoic philosophers. Apply Stoic principles in your daily life, whether in triumph or adversity.

Remember, Stoicism is a lifelong practice. It requires dedication, self-reflection, and a commitment to growth. Embrace this philosophy and let it shape your journey towards a more fulfilled and tranquil life.

Thank you for being part of this Stoic journey. May these teachings inspire and guide you as you seek inner peace and personal growth.

Made in the USA
Columbia, SC
28 September 2023

23557632R00087